2

Reading for the Gifted Student

Challenging Activities for the Advanced Learner

Written by **Danielle Denega**

Illustrations by **Viviana Garofoli**

An imprint of Sterling Children's Books

FLASH KIDS, STERLING, and the distinctive Sterling logo are registered trademarks of
Sterling Publishing Co., Inc.

Published by Sterling Publishing Co., Inc.
387 Park Avenue South, New York, NY 10016
Text and illustrations © 2005 by Flash Kids
Distributed in Canada by Sterling Publishing
c/o Canadian Manda Group, 165 Dufferin Street
Toronto, Ontario, Canada M6K 3H6
Distributed in the United Kingdom by GMC Distribution Services
Castle Place, 166 High Street, Lewes, East Sussex, England BN7 1XU
Distributed in Australia by Capricorn Link (Australia) Pty. Ltd.
P.O. Box 704, Windsor, NSW 2756, Australia

Sterling ISBN 978-1-4114-3429-5

Manufactured in Canada

Lot #:
6 8 10 9 7
02/13

For information about custom editions, special sales, premium and
corporate purchases, please contact Sterling Special Sales
Department at 800-805-5489 or specialsales@sterlingpublishing.com.

Cover image © Annabelle Breakey/Getty Images
Cover design and production by Mada Design, Inc.

Whether your student has been identified as gifted and talented or is simply a scholastic overachiever, school-assigned activities may not be challenging enough for him or her. To keep your student engaged in learning, it is important to provide reading activities that quench his or her thirst for information and allow opportunities to exercise critical thinking.

This workbook contains much more than typical reading passages and questions; it does not rely on the assumption that a gifted and talented second-grader simply requires third-grade work. Instead, the nearly 200 pages of reading passages, comprehension questions, and creative activities are calibrated to match the average reading level, analytical capacity, and subject interest of this specialized group of learners. Specifically, the vocabulary, sentence structure, and length of passages in this grade 2 workbook are set at levels normally appropriate for grades 3 and 4, but the comprehension skills increase in difficulty as the workbook progresses, starting with grade 2 curriculum standards and working through those associated with grade 3. The passages' topics are primarily nonfiction and present concepts, themes, and issues fundamental to all disciplines, including science, social studies, health, and the arts.

Question formats range from multiple choice and short answer to true-or-false, fill-in-the-blank, and much more. Also sprinkled throughout the workbook are creative activities that will encourage your student to write a story or draw a picture. Your student may check his or her work against the answer key near the end of the workbook, or you may wish to review it together, since many questions have numerous possible answers.

Reading, writing, and language skills are essential to any student's academic success. By utilizing this workbook, you are providing your gifted learner an opportunity to seek new challenges and experience learning at an advanced level.

Contents

Gary Garlic

Gary Garlic adores garlic. He eats garlic with chicken. He sprinkles garlic on popcorn. He even puts garlic on hot dogs! Gary Garlic grows garlic in his garden. After Gary chops garlic, he doesn't wash his hands. "Why wash away that glorious garlic smell?" he asks.

Gary Garlic has a cooking apron with pictures of garlic on it. He has a bobblehead doll with a garlic head. Gary Garlic also goes to the local garlic festival every year. There he samples all the garlic goodness that others have cooked up. Gary Garlic simply can't get enough garlic!

Answer the questions about the story.

1. What is Gary's favorite thing? _____

2. What is the name of another stinky food?_____

3. What types of food are mentioned in the story? Circle them all.

Baby Animals

Most baby animals have a special name. Some baby animal names are listed below.

Animal	Baby Name
Cat	Kitten
Sheep	Lamb
Kangaroo	Joey
Dog	Puppy
Elephant	Calf

Follow the directions. Use the information from the chart.

1. Color the picture of a baby elephant gray. Write its baby name underneath.

2. Color the picture of a baby cat orange. Write its baby name underneath.

3. Color the picture of a baby dog black. Write its baby name underneath.

4. Color the picture of a baby kangaroo brown. Write its baby name underneath.

Zoey's Zoo

Zoey is a young girl who lives on a deserted island with her father, George. No one else knows about their island. Zoey is seven years old. She has red hair, freckles, and brown eyes.

There are no other children on the island. But that's not a problem for Zoey!

Zoey made friends with the animals on the island. Her best friend is a lizard named Tex. Zoey and Tex are also friends with a seagull named Jon and a lemur named Bugsy. Zoey has a lot of fun with her animal buddies!

Follow the directions.

1. Write the name of the main character. _____

2. Color the drawing of the main character to show what she looks like. Then color her friends.

3. The *setting* is where a story takes place. Circle the setting of the story.

deserted island   **summer camp**   **snowy mountain**

Super Skeleton

Human bones fit together to make the skeleton. The skeleton supports the whole human body. Bones protect the organs that are inside the body. When bones work together with muscles, they also help you move.

When we are born, there are about 300 bones in our bodies. But as we grow, some of those bones fuse, or join, together. So, adult humans have only 206 bones. The largest bone in the human body is called the femur, or thighbone. The smallest bone in the body is called the stapes bone. It is located inside the ear.

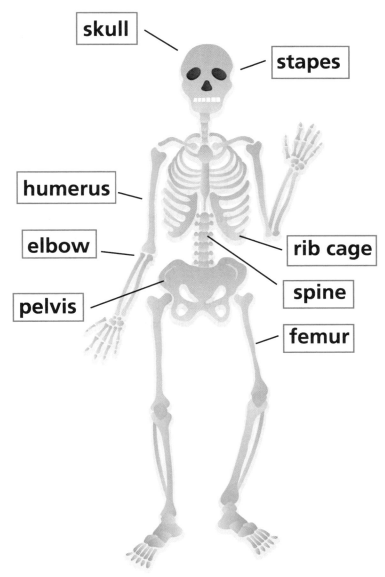

Use what you learned from the reading to fill in the blanks.

1. The largest bone in the human skeleton is the

_____.

2. The smallest bone in the body is called the

_____ bone.

3. There are about _____ bones in our bodies when we are born. When we grow up, we have only _____ bones.

Message from the Past

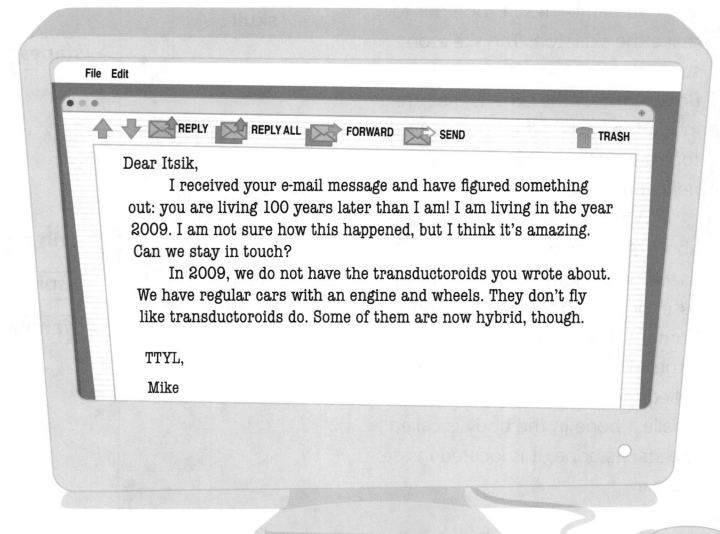

File   Edit

REPLY   REPLY ALL   FORWARD   SEND   TRASH

Dear Itsik,

     I received your e-mail message and have figured something out: you are living 100 years later than I am! I am living in the year 2009. I am not sure how this happened, but I think it's amazing. Can we stay in touch?

     In 2009, we do not have the transductoroids you wrote about. We have regular cars with an engine and wheels. They don't fly like transductoroids do. Some of them are now hybrid, though.

TTYL,

Mike

Complete each sentence about the e-mail. Write the answer on the line.

1. Mike is living in the year _____.

2. Itsik is living 100 years later than Mike, in the year _____.

3. "Transductoroids" are _____

_____

I ♥ NY

New York State is located in the northeast part of the United States. It sits along the Atlantic coast. New York State has the largest city in the country: New York City. This state produces more apples than most other states. Northern areas of New York State get more snow than many places in the country. In New York State there are many exciting places to visit, such as the Statue of Liberty and the National Baseball Hall of Fame and Museum. Here are some other facts about New York:

Date of statehood:
July 26, 1788
Abbreviation: NY
Capital: Albany
Nickname: Empire State
Area: 49,112 square miles
Motto: Ever Upward
Tree: Sugar maple
Bird: Bluebird

Follow the directions.

1. Circle the name of the state bird of New York.

2. Circle the name of the largest city in the country.

3. Circle the name of the state tree of New York.

4. Circle two places to visit in New York State.

Best Buds

Bert and Benjamin are best buds. They have been friends since they were born! Bert and Benjamin have last names that begin with the letter B.

Bert and Benjamin both love baseball and basketball. Bert and Benjamin have the same favorite foods: bananas and broccoli! Benjamin and Bert also have the same favorite bug, which is, of course, the bumblebee.

Use the words from the word bank to answer the questions about the story.

butterfly	apple	banana
soccer	spider	bumblebee
basketball	orange	hockey

1. What is a sport that Benjamin and Bert enjoy?

_____

2. What is their favorite bug?

_____

3. What is one of their favorite foods?

_____

Dibble Dabble

My favorite game to play at the lake is called Dibble Dabble. As long as you can swim well, you can play!

To begin Dibble Dabble, everyone stands on the edge of the dock. The person who is "It" has a Popsicle stick in his or her hand. That person dives deep under the water and lets go of the stick.

The other players watch the water. As soon as the stick rises to the surface, everyone jumps into the water! The player who grabs the stick wins the game. Then the winner becomes "It" and a new round of Dibble Dabble begins.

1. Number the game rules in the correct order.

_____ The winner becomes "It" and a new round of Dibble Dabble begins.

_____ "It" dives deep under the water and lets go of the stick.

_____ Everyone jumps into the water, and the player who grabs the stick wins the game.

_____ The other players watch the water.

_____ All the players stand on the edge of the dock.

2. What is one important thing to know when playing Dibble Dabble?

_____

_____

"O Canada"

Canada is north of the United States. This country is famous for hockey, beautiful landscapes, and cold weather!

Capital City	Ottawa
Location	Northern North America, above the United States
Population	33,063,000
Area	3,855,101 square miles
Language	English, French
Currency	Canadian dollars
National Anthem	"O Canada"

Answer the questions about Canada.

1. What languages are spoken in Canada?

_____

2. What is one thing Canada is famous for?

_____

3. What is the capital city of Canada?

_____

4. What are the colors of the Canadian flag?

_____

Review or Report

A book report is what it sounds like: it's a report on a book! Most book reports begin by telling the author's name and when he or she wrote it. Then a book report gives a summary of the book. The summary tells the big events in the book.

Book reviews are different from book reports. A book review tells the reader's opinion about the book. The reader will say if he or she thought the book was good or bad, and why. A book review helps other people to decide whether to read the same book.

Use what you learned from the reading to fill in the blanks.

1. A book report begins with information about the _____.

2. A book report gives a _____ of what happened in the book.

3. A book _____ tells the reader's opinion about the book.

4. A book review helps other people decide whether to

_____ the same book.

Sandy Shores

Write a story about what is happening in the picture. Use the title to guide you.

_____

_____

_____

_____

_____

_____

_____

Music Maven

James is an excellent musician. James plays the saxophone and guitar. He can play the piano better than anyone I know. James started taking music lessons when he was only four years old. By the time he was six, people told James he was a music master!

If you ask James to play something, he will make up an amazing song at that very moment. James can also hear another person's song only once and then play it exactly right. He can do it without sheet music! James is a true music maven.

Answer the questions about the story. Write the letter of the answer on the line.

1. What do you think James likes to do most? _____

    a. play baseball   **b.** play music   **c.** write poetry

2. What kind of job might James take when he grows up? _____

    a. ballerina   **b.** magician   **c.** music teacher

3. What do you think a *maven* is? _____

    a. beginner   **b.** expert   **c.** professor

Beatlemania

One of the most important music bands in history is the Beatles. The Beatles were a rock-and-roll band from Liverpool, England. The members of the band were Paul McCartney, Ringo Starr, George Harrison, and John Lennon.

The Beatles became very popular during the 1960s. People loved them so much that they would scream and faint whenever the Beatles walked onstage. This amount of excitement was given the name "Beatlemania." The Beatles had dozens of hits and became part of the Rock and Roll Hall of Fame in 1988. Sadly, the Beatles split up in 1970, but their music lives on.

Write *yes* or *no* to tell whether the sentence is the main idea of the reading.

1. The Beatles became very popular during the 1960s. _____

2. The Beatles are one of the most important music bands in history. _____

3. The Beatles were a rock-and-roll band from Liverpool, England. _____

4. People loved them so much that they would scream and faint whenever the Beatles walked onstage. _____

Rock Idol

Jasper waited for his name to be called. He was dressed in black pants and a black shirt and jacket, and he had a gold chain around his neck. When his manager called him, Jasper jogged onto the stage. The crowd was screaming his name and waving their arms in the air. Jasper grabbed the microphone and sang his greatest songs.

When the lights went down, Jasper walked offstage. "Let's do a wardrobe change, kid. You're back on in five!" Jasper's manager said. Jasper nodded and rushed off to change his outfit for the second set of songs.

Answer the questions about the story.

1. What is Jasper wearing? Color the picture.

2. What is Jasper's job? _____

3. Would you like to have Jasper's job someday? Why or why not?

_____

_____

_____

_____

_____

Ballerina Brittney

Brittney is an outstanding ballerina. She was my ballet teacher before she moved to another town. Now Brittney dances with the best dance company in the whole country! Brittney's company performed in my town this month, and I went to watch her dance.

Brittney moved beautifully across the stage. *Jeté, pirouette, arabesque*—she did all the prettiest ballet moves. Brittney wore a pink leotard and matching pink satin shoes. Her white skirt was light and airy.

Circle *fact* or *opinion* after each statement from the story.

1. Brittney is an outstanding ballerina.

              fact   **opinion**

2. Brittney wore a pink leotard and matching pink satin shoes.

              fact   **opinion**

3. Brittney moved beautifully across the stage.

              fact   **opinion**

Family Fun

Use the picture to answer the questions.

1. What things does the family smell?

_____

2. What things does the family hear?

_____

3. What things does the family touch?

_____

Marvelous Martin

Martin Luther King, Jr., was one of the most important leaders in history. He lived in Montgomery, Alabama, with his wife. King led a campaign against a bus company in Montgomery. The bus company was forcing black people to give their bus seats to white people.

In 1963, Martin Luther King, Jr., led a march in Washington, D.C. There he gave his famous "I Have a Dream" speech. In this speech, he talked about a world of people of different colors getting along with each other. In 1964, King won the Nobel Peace Prize for all of his efforts. Sadly, in 1968, Martin Luther King, Jr., was killed by a man named James Earl Ray. We celebrate the life of Martin Luther King, Jr., each year on the third Monday in January.

Write *yes* or *no* to tell whether the sentence is the main idea of the reading.

1. In 1963, Martin Luther King, Jr., led a march in Washington, D.C.

_____

2. King led a campaign against a bus company in Montgomery.

_____

3. Martin Luther King, Jr., was one of the most important leaders in history. _____

4. In 1964, King won the Nobel Peace Prize for his efforts.

_____

Melanie Smellanie

Melanie walked into the classroom with her head down. She was guided by the school's principal, who said, "Melanie, this is your teacher, Ms. Smith. Class, this is Melanie. She is new to our school. Let's make her feel welcome." Melanie could feel every set of eyes in the room staring at her. She wished she could turn around and run out the classroom door.

Ms. Smith showed Melanie to her seat. Melanie sat in the blue chair and looked straight down at her desk. "Psst!" said the boy next to her. "Is your last name Smellanie? Melanie Smellanie! Ha-ha! Melanie smells!" Melanie's face felt hot and flushed. She gulped. It was going to be a long day.

Use what you read in the story to fill in the blanks.

1. When Melanie is teased, she probably feels _____.

2. Melanie's new teacher, Ms. _____, showed her to her seat.

3. Color Melanie's chair the correct color.

Crabby Crustaceans

Crabs are a type of crustacean. Crustaceans are animals whose bodies are covered in a hard shell. Other crustaceans are lobster, crayfish, and shrimp. There are more than 4,500 kinds of crabs and almost all live in or near water. Crabs can be as small as a pea, like the pea crab. Crabs can also be much larger in size, like the Japanese spider crab. This crab has legs that span nearly 13 feet!

Crabs are *decapods*, which means they have ten limbs attached to the main part of their bodies. Eight of these ten limbs are legs. They use their legs to move sideways instead of forward. The other two limbs on a crab's body are its claws. Crabs use their claws to protect themselves and to catch food. Speaking of food, crabs will eat almost anything! They prefer to eat small fish and shellfish, but crabs will also eat seaweed, algae, and even dead plants and animals.

Follow the directions.

1. Circle the purpose of this reading.

   to persuade

   to entertain

   to give information

2. Circle the pea crab in the picture.

3. Circle the Japanese spider crab's claws in the picture.

History Lesson

Sam was really worried. He was getting his history test back today. He had baseball practice the night before the test. Sam wasn't able to study for long. He also had a hard time focusing on the test. So he wasn't surprised when he saw a huge D marked on the top of the returned test.

When Sam got home from school, his parents were not pleased. They told Sam that he was grounded for the whole weekend! Before his next history test, Sam spent a lot of time studying. He didn't want to come home with another poor grade. It worked! Sam got a B+ on the next test.

Answer the questions about the story.

1. What caused Sam to get a poor grade on his test?

_____

_____

2. What were the effects of Sam's bad grade?

_____

_____

_____

Last Day of School

The last day of each school year is both sad and exciting for Sarah. She enjoys many things about school. She loves art class and eating lunch with her friends every day. Sarah looks forward to after-school activities, such as playing soccer for her school's team.

But Sarah also really likes summertime. Then she doesn't have to do homework. She gets to sleep late every morning! Sarah takes swimming lessons and goes on a great family vacation. Sarah also spends two weeks at sleepaway camp. There she makes fun crafts and gets to see her camp friends again.

Use the clues to complete the crossword puzzle about the story.

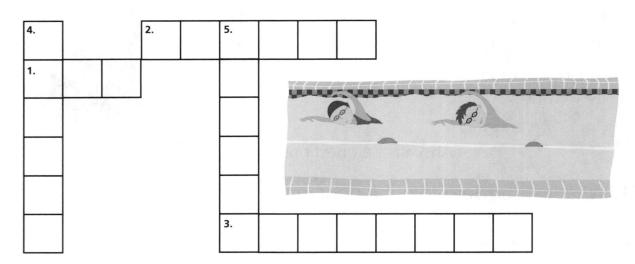

Across

1. the class Sarah likes in school

2. the sport Sarah plays after school

3. the summer lessons Sarah takes

Down

4. the people Sarah goes on summer vacation with

5. what Sarah makes at camp

Discovering Ecuador

Ecuador is a country located in South America. It sits on the coast of the Pacific Ocean. The equator crosses right through Ecuador. In fact, the word *Ecuador* is the Spanish word for "equator."

The coast of Ecuador is covered in tropical forests. In the middle of Ecuador are the Andes Mountains. The Andes are so high that some of the mountain peaks are covered in snow all year long.

The Galapagos Islands lie off the coast of Ecuador. These islands are famous for animals and plants that don't exist anywhere else in the world!

Use the words from the word bank and what you learned from the reading to fill in the blanks.

Andes	Atlantic	fish	equator
Rocky	Galapagos	Pacific	Canary

1. Ecuador sits on the coast of the _____ Ocean.

2. In Spanish, *Ecuador* means _____ .

3. The _____ Mountains are in Ecuador.

4. The _____ Islands are near Ecuador.

Great Galapagos

The Galapagos Islands are a group of islands, or *archipelago*. The Galapagos Islands are in the Pacific Ocean. This archipelago has thirteen large islands and many more small islands.

The Galapagos Islands are famous for unique animal life. Many of the animals in the Galapagos don't live anywhere else in the world! In fact, the islands get their name from the Spanish word *galápago*, which means "giant tortoise." There are eleven species, or types, of giant tortoise that live only on the Galapagos Islands.

Answer the questions about the reading. Write the letter of the answer on the line.

1. What is an *archipelago*? _____

      a. a mountain range   **b.** a group of islands   **c.** a desert

2. What does the word *unique* in paragraph 2 mean? _____

      a. the same as   **b.** different from anything else   **c.** common

3. What does the word *species* in paragraph 2 mean? _____

      a. sizes   **b.** colors   **c.** types

High Dive

Finn stood on the diving board and looked down. The blue pool below was filled with many friendly faces. The diving instructor urged Finn to make the leap. Finn inched his way closer to the edge of the diving board. He curled his toes around it and looked down again. He bent over the edge of the diving board and jumped.

It was a fun ride down! And a second or two later, Finn was plunging into the pool. The cold water felt great. He swam to the surface and shook the water from his face. "That was awesome!" he shouted. Finn's instructor and classmates were cheering. "Can I do it again?" he asked.

Circle *true* or *false* after each statement about the story.

1. Finn is learning to dive.   true   false

2. Finn hates the cold water in the pool.   true   false

3. Finn enjoyed his experience.   true   false

Clean-up Crew

Write a story about what is happening in the picture. Use the title to guide you.

_____

_____

_____

_____

_____

_____

_____

_____

Forest Friends

Forests are filled with many types of animals. Many forest animals are mammals. Mammals are creatures that have warm blood, a backbone, and fur or hair. All female mammals produce milk for feeding their young.

Animals in the forest eat lots of different foods. Animals that eat mostly plants are called *herbivores*. Deer, mice, chipmunks, and rabbits are herbivores. Other forest mammals are insect-eaters, or *insectivores*. These include moles and shrews. Forests are also home to meat-eating mammals, such as bears and mountain lions. Another term for "meateater" is *carnivore*. They eat other forest mammals!

1. Match each animal to its type.

bear	carnivore
rabbit	insectivore
mole	herbivore

2. What are four characteristics of a mammal?

_____

_____

_____

Dear John

Dear John,

What's new with you? I hope everything has been great with school and soccer. What position are you playing this season? I know you really enjoyed playing halfback last year.

I have been busy with a project for this year's science fair. I'm trying to make a volcano that really erupts! It hasn't worked so far, but I am going to keep trying. I also found out that I will be first clarinet chair in the band this year! I have been practicing a lot, so all that hard work really paid off. My music instructor is really proud of me. She told me that I'm her best student!

I can't wait to see you at Grandma's next month for the holidays. I hope she makes her chicken noodle soup, as usual. I know it's your favorite, too!

Talk to you soon,
Jenny

Answer the questions about the letter.

1. Who is writing this letter? _____

2. Who will receive this letter? _____

3. What is one thing you learn about the person writing the letter?

_____

4. What is one thing you learn about the person receiving the letter?

_____

Biscuit Bake

To make Marsha's Famous Biscuits, you will need the following ingredients:

2 cups of flour

$2\frac{1}{2}$ teaspoons of baking powder

$\frac{1}{2}$ teaspoon of salt

$\frac{1}{3}$ cup of shortening

$\frac{3}{4}$ cup of milk

Instructions:

1. Mix flour, baking powder, and salt.

2. Slowly blend in shortening until mixture is crumbly.

3. Add milk and blend until mixture is moist.

4. Lightly knead the mixture on a surface sprinkled with flour.

5. Roll dough flat until it is $\frac{3}{4}$-inch thick.

6. Cut dough with a biscuit cutter.

7. Bake on a greased pan at 475 degrees for 12 to 15 minutes.

   1. Number the steps in the correct order.

   _____ Add milk and blend until mixture is moist.

   _____ Mix flour, baking powder, and salt.

   _____ Bake on a greased pan at 475 degrees for 12 to 15 minutes.

   _____ Lightly knead the mixture on a surface sprinkled with flour.

   2. What do you think might happen if you baked the dough for only 6 minutes?

   _____

Crazy Old Bird

Just down the street, in the house with the white shutters, lives the Bird Lady. The Bird Lady got her name from the kids in the neighborhood. No one knows her real name. Everyone is afraid to ask.

What they do know is that the Bird Lady sits silent and still on her porch for hours every day. She sits so still that all the birds come and rest on her. The birds must think she is an inanimate, or unmoving, object! The birds line up across her shoulders and down her arms. They squat on her thighs and perch on her head. Sometimes, the birds even peck at her a little bit! But the Bird Lady never moves an inch.

Follow the directions.

1. Circle the sentence that tells where the Bird Lady lives.

2. Underline the sentences that explain what the Bird Lady does every day.

3. Circle the parts of the Bird Lady where the birds sit.

Veterans Day

Veterans Day is an American holiday celebrated each November 11. Veterans Day honors all veterans, who are men and women in the United States military. The have served our country in times of peace and war.

Veterans Day used to be called Armistice Day. Armistice Day recognized that World War I ended on November 11, 1918. That's why it is held on the eleventh day of the eleventh month of the year.

In 1954, the name of the holiday was changed to Veterans Day. This honored those who had also served in World War II and the Korean War. Today all veterans are honored on Veterans Day, including veterans of recent wars, such as the Iraq War.

Use what you learned from the reading to fill in the blanks.

1. Veterans Day honors people who have been a part of the United States _____.

2. On November 11, 1918, _____ ended.

3. Veterans Day used to be called _____ Day.

Middle Seat

I'm stuck in the middle car seat. This always happens to me! In the middle, there is a hump between your feet, so you have to move each foot to one side of it. But your feet take some of the foot space of the people *not* in the middle, so they kick you in the ankles.

In the middle, you have no control of the windows. Others can roll them up and roll them down, and you are at their mercy. You can also barely see out the windows. So you spend the ride staring at an endless stretch of highway ahead.

In the middle, you have no headrest. When you fall asleep, your head bobs up and down like a buoy at sea. When you wake up, your neck is tired and sore. It often takes an entire day for your neck to feel better! Next time, I am definitely calling shotgun.

Answer the questions about the story.

1. What situation is the narrator in?

_____

2. How do you think the narrator feels about this situation?

_____

3. How do you know?

_____

4. How do you feel when you are in the same situation?

_____

Camping Companions

We picked a flat, dry area for setting up camp. We unloaded our packs and divided the duties. Jack would pitch the tent with Sam. Trevor and Adam would search the woods for firewood. Then Jesse would make a fire. "Melvin, after dinner hang the food from a tree, so the bears don't get to it," Sam told me. Andrew was responsible for unpacking the drinks from the cooler packs and helping Jack and Sam with the tent.

An hour later, Jack, Sam, Trevor, Adam, Jesse, Andrew, and I curled up in our sleeping bags after zipping the tent closed. "Who is supposed to put out the fire?" I asked. We all looked at each other and shrugged. I sighed and said, "Fine, I'll do it."

Match each picture to the correct name or names from the story.

Trevor and Adam

Melvin

Jack and Sam

Jesse

Tall Towers

The world's tallest buildings are so high that they seem to scrape the sky. That's why we call them skyscrapers. Skyscrapers can be hundreds of stories high. Built upward, skyscrapers hold a lot of inside space on a small area of ground.

Skyscrapers are usually built from steel. Steel is much stronger than most other building materials. A steel frame allows tall buildings to endure the strong winds at such great heights.

Some of the most famous skyscrapers in our country are the Empire State Building in New York City and the Sears Tower in Chicago. The first skyscraper ever constructed was the Home Insurance Building in Chicago. It was completed in 1885 and was only ten stories high. That does not seem very tall compared to today's giant buildings!

Answer the questions about the reading.

1. Why are skyscrapers often made of steel?

_____

2. Name one American skyscraper.

_____

3. Why can skyscrapers be built on a small area of ground?

_____

Diva Darcy

Darcy went to sleepaway camp for the first time. It was not at all what she was used to! Darcy had to sleep in a sleeping bag on a small cot, rather than in her king-size bed at home. Darcy had to walk a half mile to the mess hall for breakfast. At home, the butler would bring her breakfast while she was in bed. Darcy had to clean up the entire mess hall after dinner one night. Darcy even had to scrub the toilets. She certainly never had to do that at home!

Darcy often complained about her camp duties. Her bunkmates always rolled their eyes. "You're such a diva, Darcy!" they'd tell her. But Darcy didn't care what they called her. Darcy just wanted to go back home!

Answer the questions about the story.

1. Name four things Darcy had to do at sleepaway camp.

_____

_____

_____

_____

2. What do you think Darcy's nickname means?

_____

_____

3. Do you think Darcy enjoyed sleepaway camp? Why or why not?

_____

_____

Crafty Kitty

Susan hadn't seen Oscar for hours. Oscar was Susan's orange and white kitten. Susan checked everywhere for him. She peered under the beds. She looked inside the cabinets. Susan even checked in the clothes dryer. Oscar was nowhere to be found.

When Susan went to bed that night, she felt worried and scared for Oscar. She wondered if something bad had happened to her kitten. Susan sighed and switched off the lamp next to her bed. She snuggled under the covers, but she knew it would be hard to sleep that night. At that very moment, Susan felt something move near her feet. She heard the quilt rustle. She threw back the covers. "Oscar!" she shouted. "You crafty kitty! How did you get under there?" Oscar just purred and curled up next to Susan's pillow.

Number the events in the correct order.

_____ Oscar just purred and curled up next to Susan's pillow.

_____ Susan checked everywhere for Oscar.

_____ Susan hadn't seen Oscar for hours.

_____ When Susan went to bed that night, she felt worried and scared for Oscar.

Kitty in the City

Lucy was a city kitty. She lived in an apartment building with her owner, Marina. Marina adopted her when Lucy looked like a tiny ball of fur. But now Lucy was a full-grown cat. And she had never been free in the city until yesterday. Lucy snuck out! She squeezed out the door and scampered down the stairs. When someone opened the front door, Lucy ran outside.

Lucy was surrounded by tall trees and even taller buildings. She heard construction noises, traffic, and people talking all around her. Terrible smells like trash and car fumes crept up her nose. The humans nearly trampled her. Cars almost ran her over! Lucy hid in an alley. Maybe the city was no place for a kitty!

Answer the questions about the story.

1. What did Lucy see in the city? Circle those words in the story.

2. What did Lucy hear in the city? Underline those words in the story.

3. What did Lucy smell in the city? Box those words in the story.

The Four Seasons

A year is divided into four seasons: winter, spring, summer, and fall, or autumn. What creates these divisions? The sun and the earth do! The earth orbits, or revolves in a circle, around the sun. It takes a year for the earth to orbit the sun. Each season happens because of what position the earth is in.

Each season has different air temperatures and amounts of daylight. In North America, summer days are the longest and warmest of the year. Then summer changes to fall, and the weather cools. The amount of daylight lessens. By winter, the temperatures are cold and there are not many daylight hours. Moving into spring, the days become longer again and the temperatures warm up.

Unscramble the words mentioned in the reading.

1. nsu _____

2. ringps _____

3. evrlove _____

4. itdalygh _____

5. ssonea _____

Grown-up Troubles

Sometimes I hate being a kid. So last night I wished to be a grown-up. This morning, I woke up with scruff on my chin and I had to shave my face. That wasn't so easy! Then I had to drive a car. I almost hit a sign, and I was late for work. All day I felt like my necktie was choking me.

After work, there was no food prepared. I had to try to make dinner. I cooked pasta but dropped the bowl on the floor. What a mess! I sure hope I'm a kid again in the morning!

Answer the questions about the story.

1. Have you ever thought life might be better as an adult? Why or why not?

_____

_____

_____

2. What are three adult things the narrator has to do?

_____

_____

_____

Mosquitoes Bite

Do you think that polar bears are dangerous? How about rhinoceroses? Yes, these creatures will hurt a human. You don't want to run into one of those in the wild. But there is one creature that is much more dangerous to humans: the mosquito. This flying pest is actually the most dangerous creature on the planet.

Mosquitoes are dangerous because of their amazing ability to spread disease. If a bug carrying a disease bites a human, he or she can become infected with the disease, too. Mosquitoes can spread diseases such as malaria, yellow fever, and West Nile virus. In areas with a lot of mosquitoes, people can protect themselves by using bug repellents and mosquito nets. They can also get shots to guard against most of the diseases mosquitoes carry.

Use what you learned from the reading to fill in the blanks.

1. Mosquitoes are more dangerous than a _____ bear or a rhinoceros.

2. Mosquitoes spread diseases such as _____ fever.

3. Doctors can give _____ to guard against diseases mosquitoes carry.

Donna Downer

Donna is a real downer. When you ask Donna how she is, she always replies, "So-so." Donna never wants to go outside because it's always "too" something. It's "too hot," "too cold," "too rainy," or "too sunny." Donna never feels well. If Donna doesn't have a headache, then she has a cold. One day, Donna even complained that her hair hurt!

Donna does not like ice cream. Donna does not like the zoo. Donna doesn't care for kittens or movies or hopscotch. Donna can't stand cotton candy, the beach, or bicycle rides. Donna cannot be pleased, no matter how hard anyone tries.

One day I asked Donna, "Why are you such a downer?" Donna looked at me with great surprise and said, "Why, whatever do you mean?"

"Donna, you don't like anything or anyone. You're always feeling down and you make me feel down, too."

Donna thought for a moment and replied, "I like you. Doesn't that count for something?" I sighed and smiled at Donna. She may be a downer, but she's still my friend.

Answer the questions about the story.

1. What are three things that Donna does not like?

_____

_____

2. Do you think that Donna would like the park? Why or why not?

_____

3. What is one thing that Donna does like? _____

Animals in Danger

Experts estimate that more than 1,000 types of animals are endangered or threatened worldwide. This means that these animals are at risk of dying out. When an animal completely dies out, it becomes extinct. African elephants and tigers are only two of the wonderful animals in danger of becoming extinct.

Humans are the greatest threat to animals. By building on their homes, we destroy them. We pollute their food and water sources. Humans even hunt and kill endangered animals. But there are programs and organizations, such as the World Wildlife Fund, that work to solve these problems. Supporting these organizations is one way people can help solve this problem.

Circle the correct answer after each statement from the reading.

1. Humans hunt and kill endangered animals.

                              fact   **opinion**

2. Experts estimate that more than 1,000 types of animals are endangered or threatened worldwide.

                              fact   **opinion**

3. What do you think the author is trying to do in this reading? Circle all that apply.

               entertain   **inform**   **persuade**

Wetland Habitat

Wetlands are areas of land that are wet for at least part of every year. Sometimes wetlands are completely covered in water. At other times the water is quite shallow. Bogs, swamps, and marshes are examples of wetlands. Wetlands serve several important functions but they are being destroyed, and they need to be saved.

Wetlands are home to large numbers of wildlife. By destroying wetland areas, we are destroying these plants and animals. In fact, many threatened and endangered species in the United States live in wetland habitats.

Wetlands are also important because of their water. Wetlands store and clean the water we depend on. After a long rain or flood, wetland areas hold onto that water like a sponge. Then the water is released slowly, so it's available when we need it. Without wetlands, our water supply would run low.

Answer the questions about the reading.

1. What are three examples of wetlands?

_____

_____

_____

2. Why are wetlands useful to people?

_____

3. What is one effect of destroying wetlands?

_____

_____

Rita Recycles

Rita recycles everything! Rita likes to use things again. Instead of throwing them away, she knows that she is helping to save the planet. Rita understands that using recycled materials is better for the earth. They cost less and need less energy to make than new materials do. Rita also knows that recycling reduces pollution and the amount of land needed to store trash.

In school, Rita puts every sheet of paper into the recycling bin. She also does this with newspapers, magazines, and cardboard at home. Her notebooks are made from recycled paper. Her backpack is made from recycled fabric. And her water bottle is made from recycled plastic!

Find these words from the story in the word puzzle below.

recycled   **pollution**   **trash**   **newspapers**   **earth**

R	S	N	E	W	S	P	A	P	E	R	S
E	A	R	T	H	B	H	A	D	P	R	Z
C	H	D	R	S	X	S	L	E	O	B	T
Y	Q	U	A	U	D	A	N	E	L	I	X
C	N	B	S	N	L	O	A	C	L	V	T
L	B	X	H	L	T	H	Z	A	U	Q	U
E	K	E	E	N	U	G	F	S	T	T	U
D	D	P	U	C	S	R	H	T	I	D	N
O	A	M	U	D	W	G	N	O	O	N	V
C	E	D	N	X	R	S	I	R	N	U	S

Saving Water

Earth is covered in water, but most of it is seawater that is too salty to drink. Humans need freshwater to survive. Plants and animals also need it to live. But only 3 percent of earth's water is freshwater. And most of that freshwater is trapped in frozen glaciers and ice caps. That doesn't leave much available freshwater, and we are running out quickly. It is important for humans to conserve, or save, water.

To keep our water supply going, we need to use water no faster than the rate that it can be replaced. We also need to use less water so that we can conserve energy. "Handling" water, which means pumping, delivering, and cleaning it, uses a large amount of energy (another thing that is running out!).

Saving water also means we will be saving plants and animals. If we use less water, water habitats may not die out. This is called habitat conservation. So think about ways in which you and your community can use less water and take those actions now!

Answer the questions about the reading. Circle the answer.

1. What are all the reasons why the author wrote this?

to entertain readers   to inform readers   to persuade readers

2. How much of earth's water is freshwater?

13 percent   33 percent   3 percent

3. What is an example of "handling" water?

pouring it in a glass   pumping it   splashing it in the ocean

Energy Conservation

There are many ways to conserve, or save, energy. To start, use less electricity at home. Turn off electrical items, such as your computer, when you're not using them. Use low-energy lightbulbs. Take short, cool showers.

You can also save energy by eating differently. It takes energy to make and transport food and water. If you eat food grown near where you live, little energy is used to get the food to the local store and then to your house. Also, drink tap water instead of bottled water. It takes a lot of energy to make plastic water bottles, ship them all over the country, and then destroy or recycle them. So turn on the tap the next time you are thirsty. Finally, get moving! Walking or riding a bike to get somewhere is another way to conserve the energy a car uses.

Place a check next to the main idea of the reading.

_____ It takes energy to make and transport food and water.

_____ Turn off electrical items, such as your computer, when you're not using them.

_____ There are many ways to conserve, or save, energy.

Margo's Math

At the store, Margo helped her mom figure out the cost of their groceries. Apples were four for $1, and they got eight. Cranberries and grapes were $2 per bag, and they pulled one bag of each from the shelf.

Margo's mom saw a sign that said pickles were on sale: $\frac{1}{2}$ off of $3.00! They put a jar in the shopping cart. Next, Margo ran to the candy aisle and saw that her favorite gummy candies were $1 per pound. She carefully measured two pounds.

Finally, they went to the front of the store to pay for their groceries. The woman behind the register told them they would get $1 off their total because Margo was a student.

Answer the questions about the story.

1. How many apples did Margo and her mother buy?

_____

2. How much did the bag of grapes cost? _____

3. How much did Margo's favorite candy cost per pound?

_____

4. What was the total amount that they paid for the groceries?

_____

Park Picture

The amusement park was full of people of all colors: brown, black, white and pink. There was a vendor selling fluffy, pink cotton candy. Another vendor was selling buttery yellow popcorn.

A superhero with a blue and red cape was posing for photos with kids. Above him, a green and purple roller coaster was zooming by. The passengers were screaming!

Color the picture to match the description in the story.

Life Changes

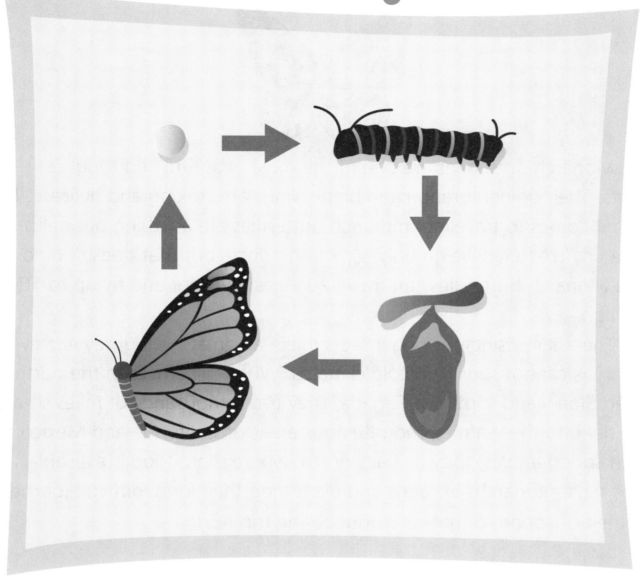

Use the diagram to answer the questions.

1. What hatches from a butterfly egg? Circle its picture.

2. What emerges from the chrysalis? Box its picture.

3. What is the first step in the life cycle of a butterfly? Underline its picture.

Majestic Monarchs

Monarch butterflies are one of the most beautiful and toughest insects. Their golden orange and black wings are striking and delicate. But, when it comes to traveling, monarch butterflies are anything but delicate. These tiny creatures weigh only $\frac{1}{50}$ of an ounce, but that doesn't hold them back. Monarch butterflies can travel 20 miles per hour and fly up to 10,000 feet high.

These surprisingly strong insects make an amazing journey each year. Monarchs cannot survive in cold climates. When fall arrives in the northern United States and southern Canada, they travel thousands of miles south. They head to the warmer, mountainous areas of California and Mexico. When spring arrives, they fly back north, where more food is available. Sadly, most monarchs lay eggs and die during their long, difficult journey. But their offspring, or babies, continue the trip north.

Write *fact* or *opinion* after each statement from the reading.

1. These tiny creatures weigh only $\frac{1}{50}$ of an ounce. _____

2. Monarch butterflies are one of the most beautiful and toughest insects. _____

3. Their golden orange and black wings are striking and delicate. _____

4. Monarchs cannot survive in cold climates. _____

Pen Pal

Dear Pierre,

How is Paris these days? I hope the weather has been pleasant. Spring hasn't been too warm here yet. Besides going to school and baseball practice, I started to learn a new musical instrument. My brother is teaching me to play the guitar! It's really difficult. Can you play any musical instruments?

I've been trying to learn French, too. I'd like to write to you in your own language one day. So far I have learned to say, "Bonjour! Ça va?" which means, "Hello! How are you?" but you know that already! I can also ask where the bathrooms are: "Excusez-moi, oú sont les toilettes?" which makes my brother laugh every time because of the word toilettes! Au revoir!

Shareef

Try to say the French phrases from the letter. Then write what they mean.

1. Bonjour! Ça va? [bohw-juhr! sah-vah?]

_____

2. Excusez-moi, où sont les toilettes? [eks-cyooz-eh-mwah, ooh sohn lay twahlet?]

_____

United States Capitol

The United States Capitol is located in Washington, D.C. It sits on Capitol Hill. The interior space of the building is about 4 acres and its lawn covers about 155 acres. Nearly the entire building is made of marble. That is one big, expensive place!

A doctor named William Thornton originally designed the Capitol. George Washington himself laid its cornerstone on September 18, 1793.

There are many important sections of the Capitol. The first is the Rotunda, which is directly under the dome of the building. Then there are the Senate Chamber, which is in the north wing, and the House Chamber, located in the south wing. There is also the President's Room as well as the National Statuary Hall, which contains statues of famous Americans.

Answer the questions about the reading.

1. Where does the Capitol sit?

_____

2. When was the building's cornerstone laid?

_____

3. Who designed the Capitol?

_____

4. What are two important parts of the building?

_____

Icy Treats

How to Make Juice Pops

1. Take out a container of your favorite juice. It could be orange juice, cranberry juice, apple juice, or grape juice. A mixed flavored drink will work, too.

2. Fill an empty ice cube tray with the juice.

3. Tightly seal the entire tray with plastic wrap.

4. Place one toothpick in the center of each cube by poking a hole through the plastic. The plastic wrap will hold the toothpick upright.

5. Place the tray carefully into the freezer. Leave until the juice cubes are frozen solid.

   If you do not have plastic wrap, you can still make juice pops. Just freeze the juice cubes a little, and then place the toothpicks into them. Return the tray to the freezer until the cubes are solid.

Number the steps in the correct order.

_____ Place the tray carefully into the freezer.

_____ Tightly seal the entire tray with plastic wrap.

_____ Place one toothpick in the center of each cube by poking a hole through the plastic.

_____ Fill an empty ice cube tray with the juice.

Summer Fun

As you read the story, fill in each blank with any word from the correct part of speech. Have fun!

After dark one summer night, all the neighborhood kids played

_____ and _____ in the glow of
   VERB   VERB

_____ bugs. _____ was the seeker and counted
   ADJECTIVE   NOUN

to twenty. The rest of the group _____ scattered to all corners
                                      ADVERB

of the _____. Everyone searched for the _____
           NOUN   ADJECTIVE

hiding place. I ran back to my own house. There was one place where I

knew I would be well hidden.

I pulled my body up into the _____ until I was out of
                                  NOUN

sight. Its _____ branches and leaves sheltered me from the
              ADJECTIVE

_____. There I sat and waited. My _____ was
   NOUN   NOUN

shallow and sweat rolled down my back.

_____ , I heard the sounds of approaching footsteps. "I
   ADVERB

can _____ you! You're it!" a _____ said from
       VERB   NOUN

below me. I was found!

Memory Making

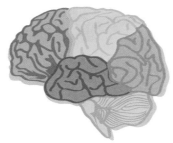

The human brain stores two types of memories: short term and long term. The hippocampus is the part of the brain that decides what type each memory will be.

Things you see, hear, smell, touch, and taste are processed in your short-term memory for a few moments. It isn't important to remember what color socks you wore yesterday, so your hippocampus makes that a short-term memory, which is soon forgotten.

When the hippocampus decides that a memory is important, it will make that information stick around as a long-term memory. It's important to remember not to touch the blade of a sharp knife. After you feel the pain, your hippocampus decides that you should remember not to do it again. This becomes a long-term memory.

Answer the questions about the reading.

1. What part of the brain is responsible for memory?

_____

2. Can you think of another example of a short-term memory?

_____

3. Can you think of another example of a long-term memory?

_____

Curious Canine

Write your own ending to this story.

Baxter is a very curious puppy. He is always checking out everything he finds. But then he gets himself into trouble! One day, Baxter approached a skunk. He had never met a skunk before, so he thought he would say hello. The skunk did not like Baxter's friendly gesture, and Baxter got sprayed.

Today, Baxter noticed wonderful smells coming from the kitchen. He ran in to see what was happening. Baxter spied a huge turkey, cooked to perfection, on the dining table. Baxter knew that the turkey was the wonderful smell, so he jumped up onto the table to get a little closer.

_____

_____

_____

_____

The Nose Knows

As you read the story, fill in the blanks using the words from the word bank.

> smell   bark   humans   tracking   hiding   five

    Tracking dogs are trained to track, or hunt, things down. Police and the military use them. Tracking dogs are usually looking for missing or _____ people. Tracking dogs are trained to follow the scent of a person. Once the dog locates the person with the right scent, the dog lets its human handler know. The dog will _____ or walk around in a circle.

    _____ dogs are very good at their jobs because of their amazing sense of _____. There are tiny scent receptors inside the noses of dogs and humans. These scent receptors tell the brain what a scent is. Humans have _____ million to fifteen million scent receptors in their noses. But dogs have 125 to 250 million! All those extra receptors make dogs better at smelling than _____. The part of the brain that identifies smells is also much larger in a dog than in a human. Their noses sure know when they smell something!

Sailor Sam

"It's time to go on a boat ride," Sam's dad, Jackson, proclaims. Sam looks up with delight and begins to drool. Sam watches Jackson pack up the cooler, slip on a jacket, and crown his head with his captain's hat.

Sam jogs down the dock. Jackson pulls the white-and-red lobster boat called the *Marsha Dawn* closer to the dock. Then they both jump on board. As they cruise, Sam hangs his head off the side of the boat and lets the wind blow back his hair. He sticks his tongue out and tries to catch some of the salty, splashing water in his mouth.

At the end of their boat ride, Sam waits patiently as his dad docks the boat. When they are close to the dock, Sam jumps off and runs to the first tree he can find. He needs to use the bathroom.

Match each picture to its correct name from the story.

Marsha Dawn

Jackson

Sam

Top Dog

In 2005, the American Kennel Club ranked the following dogs. They are the ten most popular dogs registered in their organization.

Breed	Rank	Number Registered
Labrador Retriever	1	137,867
Golden Retriever	2	48,509
Yorkshire Terrier	3	47,238
German Shepherd	4	45,014
Beagle	5	42,592
Dachshund	6	38,566
Boxer	7	37,268
Poodle	8	31,638
Shih Tzu	9	28,087
Miniature Schnauzer	10	24,144

Use the chart to match each dog breed to its number. The number could be its rank or how many were registered.

Shih Tzu   **137,867**

Beagle   **37,268**

Labrador Retriever   **5**

Boxer   **9**

Dog Lover

My friend Mike loves dogs more than anyone I know. Mike has had a dog since he was four years old. Mike and his dog Dozer are always together. Mike takes Dozer out for a long walk every day after school. On weekends, Mike plays with Dozer at the park. Dozer sleeps in Mike's bed. And every morning Dozer greets Mike with a wet, sloppy kiss!

This summer, Mike volunteered at the local animal shelter. He fed, walked, and bathed the abandoned and stray dogs. He also made sure that each one got plenty of affection and playtime. In addition, Mike works at events that raise money for the care of abandoned dogs.

Answer the questions about the story.

1. What do you think Mike's favorite thing is?

_____

2. What job do you think Mike may take when he grows up?

_____

3. What do you think Mike would do if he found a stray dog in his yard?

_____

4. How do you think Dozer and the shelter dogs feel about Mike?

_____

Maggie's Gift

Draw a line from each paragraph to the picture that shows it.

1.   Yesterday Maggie received the best gift she could have ever imagined. There was only one box, but inside were a collar, a leash, and a chew bone. She would be getting the one thing she had wanted for years. Maggie was finally allowed to get a dog!

2.   On the long drive to the animal shelter, Maggie began thinking of names. She had so many good ones in mind! At the shelter, Maggie looked around for puppies. But all she saw were adult dogs. The volunteer at the shelter explained, "All of the puppies we had were adopted right before Christmas. But there are plenty of other dogs that need good homes." Maggie bowed her head and looked at the ground. She had her heart set on a puppy.

3.   But that's when a joyful and fluffy bundle of love came running toward Maggie. The shelter volunteer picked up the dog and said that she had just come in that day. "She's already eight months old, but I think she's wonderful and thought you might, too." Maggie knelt down and felt warm wetness wash across her face. She smiled and petted the dog. "I think I'll name her Sierra," she said.

Paula's Problem

Paula couldn't focus at school today. She kept thinking about what she was going to do about her puppy, Pugsly. At breakfast that morning, Paula's mom told her, "That Pugsly is a problem! If he does not pass his puppy school classes, we will have to find another home for him."

Pugsly was failing his puppy school classes. When the dog trainer told him to sit, Pugsly chased after a squirrel. When the trainer told him to come, Pugsly rolled around on his back. When the trainer instructed him to stay, Pugsly ran over and licked her face!

Paula thought about her problem all day long. When she arrived home from school, Paula told her mom, "I just can't stand the thought of giving up my puppy. So I will help him learn to behave." Then Paula practiced Pugsly's commands with him every day.

By the end of the month, Pugsly was performing much better in puppy class. He even got a gold star for being the most improved puppy!

Answer the questions about the story.

1. The main character in this story has a problem. What is her problem?

_____

2. What did you learn about Paula from the words she says, which is called *dialogue*?

_____

3. How did Paula solve her problem?

_____

4. How do you think Paula felt when Pugsly received a gold star?

_____

Chores Are a Snore

After dinner, Erik has to do chores. "No TV before chores. No video games before chores," his mother says.

Erik clears the dishes from the table. He returns the milk to the refrigerator. He drops the used napkins in the hamper. He sweeps the crumbs from under the table. "Am I done now, Mom? Can I go play Mac Attack?" he asks.

"Yes," his mother says. "You have done your share. Thank you."

Erik goes to his room. He begins to play the video game, but he keeps losing. "I would be better at this game if I had more practice," he thinks to himself. "Why can't my mom just do the chores?"

Erik's mother walks into his room. She says, "I do all of the shopping, all of the laundry, all of the cooking, and all of the driving. It's a lot of work. I need help from the whole family."

Erik is stunned. "How did she know what I was thinking?" he wonders.

Answer the questions about the story.

1. What chores does Erik perform? Circle them in the story.

2. How does Erik feel about chores? _____

3. Why does Erik need to do chores? _____

_____

4. How would you feel if someone could tell what you were thinking?

_____

Counting Clouds

Clouds are nothing more than clumps of millions of tiny water drops or ice crystals. Before clouds form, water changes from a liquid into a gas, called water vapor. When warm air is full of water vapor, it rises up and cools down. The water vapor turns back into a liquid again, which leaves tiny drops, or droplets, in the air. These droplets are what make clouds. Clouds are usually high above earth's surface. But sometimes they are very close to the ground. Then they are called fog or mist.

Clouds come in three main forms: cumulus, stratus, and cirrus. Cumulus clouds are puffy looking. A few cumulus clouds in the sky usually mean the weather is pleasant. But many, heavy-looking cumulus clouds could mean a thunderstorm is coming. Stratus clouds are flat and resemble a bedsheet. Clouds like these form when the weather is warm and possibly rainy. Cirrus clouds look wispy and are the highest in the sky. Cirrus clouds are often full of ice crystals and can mean a storm is coming.

Complete each sentence about the reading. Circle the answer.

1. Cumulus clouds usually look _____.

        puffy   **tiny**   **dark**

2. The word *resemble* in paragraph 2 means _____.

        smells like   **looks like**   **is a**

3. Clouds are usually high above the _____ of earth.

        center   **middle**   **surface**

Colors of Light

Light is a source of energy that is visible. Many people think that light is white, but that's not really true. There is no such thing as white light! The scientist Isaac Newton discovered this fact.

Newton found that a ray of light will bend when it passes from one clear thing, like air, into another clear thing, like water. When the light hits the air again, it bends a second time. This bending of light is called refraction. Newton discovered that refracted light makes many different colors appear: red, orange, yellow, green, blue, indigo, and violet. All of these visible colors come together to make up light!

Newton's discovery also explains why we see rainbows. After it rains and the sun comes out, sunlight enters the raindrops. That light is refracted, and then refracted again when it leaves the raindrops. The light appears as a rainbow of colors.

Write *true* or *false* after each statement about the reading.

1. The bending of light is called refraction. _____

2. Light is a source of energy that we can see. _____

3. Pink is one of the colors that make up visible light. _____

4. We see rainbows because of light refraction. _____

5. *Visible* means "not able to be seen." _____

Ian on the Island

Ian woke up and was confused. He was soaking wet and covered in sand. Water lapped against his body. He stood up, brushed the sand off his face, and looked around. Ian saw a forest of palm trees, tropical birds, and coconuts on the ground. Then Ian saw something that made him gulp. His boat was shredded to pieces on the shore. *Oh, no,* he thought, *I'm stranded here.*

Draw what happens next in this story.

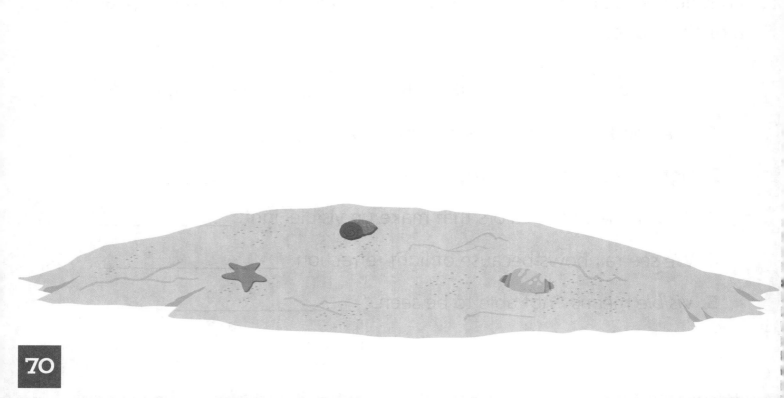

Merry Men

Long ago and deep in Sherwood Forest lived a fearless outlaw named Robin Hood. Robin could use a bow and arrow well. He lived a life of adventure with his group of friends called Merry Men. They had unusual names like Little John and Friar Tuck.

Robin Hood had enemies: Prince John, the Sheriff of Nottingham, and Sir Guy of Gisbourne. They were rich, cruel leaders whom Robin did not respect. He spent his time fighting against their tyranny.

Together, Robin and his band of Merry Men stole things. But Robin Hood and his Merry Men were not ordinary thieves. Robin Hood was a man of the people. He felt that it was wrong for the rich to have so much, while the poor suffered and had very little. So he stole from the rich and passed on the stolen goods to the poor.

Stories about the adventures of Robin Hood have been told for more than 600 years. We don't know where fact ends and fiction begins in the legend of Robin Hood, but he is always called a hero.

Answer the questions about the story. Write the letter of the answer on the line.

1. The word *tyranny* in paragraph 2 means _____.

    a. cannons   **b.** armies of ants   **c.** unfair powers

2. A *legend* is _____.

    a. a story handed down from earlier times

    b. a sword handed down from earlier times

    c. a talk given to an audience

3. Do you think Robin Hood was a hero? Why or why not?

_____

_____

Title Time

Read the story. Think of a title for the story and write it on the line.

_____

Malcolm laced up his skates and slid on his gloves. He pulled the front of his mask down over his face and picked up his hockey stick. He glided out onto the ice, followed by the rest of the starting lineup. The roar of the crowd was deafening.

Malcolm searched the crowd and saw his dad holding up a sign that said "Go Bullets!" His dad gave him a thumbs-up when Malcolm caught his eye. Malcolm took his position in the goal and waited for the whistle. The whole season had led up to this night. He knew that this would have to be the best game he had ever played.

Write what you think happens next.

_____

_____

_____

_____

_____

_____

_____

About an Ant's Body

An ant's head contains its eyes. Each of these is like many small eyes in one. These special eyes allow ants to see things that are moving. Extending from an ant's head are its feelers. The feelers enable an ant to smell and communicate with other ants. In the front of an ant's head are the pinchers. Ants use their pinchers to carry food, dig, and defend themselves against enemies.

An ant's six legs are attached to the trunk of its body. Its sharp claws help it climb and cling to things. Finally, an ant's poison sac is located in the area called the metasoma. Many types of ants also have stingers in this part of their body.

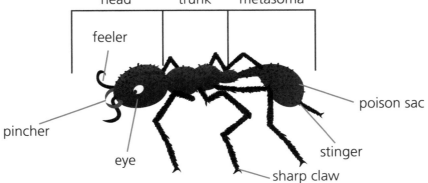

Answer the questions about the reading and the diagram.

1. Where are an ant's feelers?

_____

2. What do ants use their pinchers for?

_____

3. What is the purpose of an ant's claws?

_____

4. What is the rear portion of an ant's body called?

_____

The Princess and the _____

NOUN

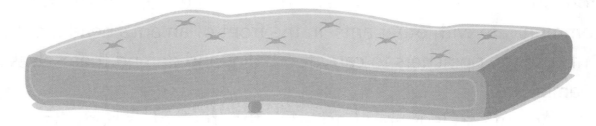

As you read the story, fill in each blank with any word from the correct part of speech. Have fun!

Once upon a time, a _____ princess traveled to a
_{ADJECTIVE}
_____ town. When she arrived, the princess was
ADJECTIVE
_____, but she didn't have a place to stay that night. The
ADJECTIVE
princess knocked on the _____ of a nice-looking house. A
NOUN
handsome _____ answered. The _____ offered
NOUN   NOUN
the princess a bed, but she could not _____ a wink that
VERB
night. The princess tossed and turned until the _____ rose
NOUN
the next day. The princess told the mother of the kind _____
NOUN
about her _____ night's sleep. The mother smiled at the
ADJECTIVE
princess and said, "Only a true princess would _____ and
VERB
_____ the whole night through just because of a pea
VERB
underneath her mattress!" "Indeed, I am a _____ ," the
NOUN
princess responded. "Did I forget to mention that?"

What's the Matter?

Matter is a scientific term for anything that takes up space. So nearly everything in the universe has matter! Matter can have three forms, which are called *states*. The three states are solid, liquid, and gas.

The main feature of a solid is that it doesn't change shape. But liquid matter is much different. A liquid will change shape to fill the bottom of the container into which it is poured. Like a liquid, a gas will change shape. But the particles of a gas will expand to completely fill any container.

Did you know that matter can change its state? Most materials are solids at low temperatures, liquids at medium temperatures, and gases at high temperatures. So if the temperature of matter changes a lot, its state can change. For example, when its temperature is very low, water is a solid, called ice. When the temperature is warmed up, ice becomes water, which is a liquid. If the temperature of water gets very high, it turns to vapor, which is a gas.

Complete each sentence about the reading. Circle the letter of the answer.

1. The three states of matter are _____ .
   a. solid, liquid, and gas.
   b. nitrogen, oxygen, and carbon dioxide.
   c. milk, water, and juice.

2. Solids _____ .
   a. will fill up any container.
   b. don't want to change shape.
   c. never change state.

3. Most matter is a gas at _____.
   a. high temperatures.
   b. low temperatures.
   c. medium temperatures.

4. When water is heated to a very high temperature, it _____.
   a. becomes ice.
   b. becomes water.
   c. becomes vapor.

Rain Forest Ralph

Ralph dragged himself through the rain forest. The air was sticky and hot. Sweat poured down Ralph's face. He sipped water from his canteen. Soon it would be empty, but Ralph couldn't worry about that now. He was lost in the jungle and needed to find his way out.

Above him, the trees were full of life. A parrot cawed and startled Ralph. He looked up and saw a python slithering dangerously close to his head. Ralph jumped away and came face-to-face with a spider monkey. Ralph stared at the creature, but then it swung away from him.

Ralph pulled out his map. It was time to check it again. He studied the wrinkled, faded page. He couldn't tell in which direction he was going anymore. Ralph tried to figure out what to do next. Just then a capybara, the world's largest rodent, ran by his feet. Ralph screamed and leaped back. "I have to get out of here," Ralph said to himself.

Draw a scene from the story.

Cultural Connection

Native Americans, or American Indians, were the first people who lived in North America. There were many different groups of Native Americans spread around the continent. Each group lived within its own cultural area. A culture is the way of life of a group of people. The map below shows the main Native American cultural areas in the United States and which groups lived in them.

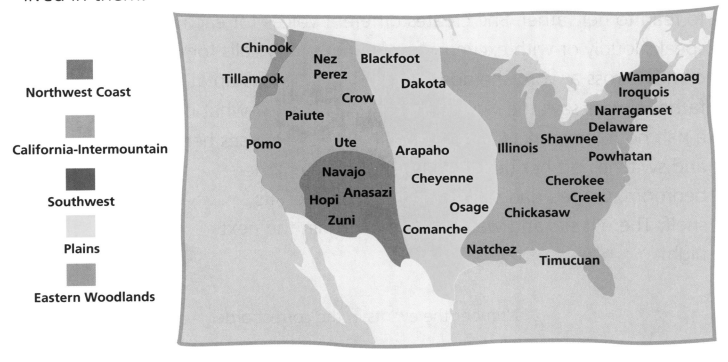

Use the reading and the map to answer the questions.

1. How many different Native American cultural areas appear on this map?

_____

2. What is the red cultural area on the map called?

_____

3. Name three types of Native Americans who lived in the Eastern Woodlands cultural area.

_____

Bedtime Ritual

Claire's favorite time of the day is bedtime. After dinner and chores, Claire climbs the stairs to put on her pajamas, brush her teeth, and wash her face. Next, she goes to her bookshelf and chooses a book. She calls her father into her room. Then she snuggles herself under her comforter. She props up her pillows and opens the book to where she left off.

When Claire's dad comes in, he sits next to her and listens. Claire loves to read to her father. She creates different voices for each character. She speaks loudly or with excitement when the story calls for it. When Claire comes across a word she does not know, she looks up at her father. Her father always says the word correctly and tells her what it means. After a half hour, he marks Claire's page in the book, kisses her good night, and switches off her bedside lamp. As he leaves her bedroom, Claire's dad places the book back on its shelf. There it sits and waits to be read again the next night.

Number the events in the correct order.

_____ She calls her father into her room.

_____ After a half hour, he marks Claire's page in the book, kisses her good night, and switches off her bedside lamp.

_____ She props up her pillows and opens the book to where she left off.

_____ After dinner and chores, Claire climbs the stairs to put on her pajamas, brush her teeth, and wash her face.

Singing in Key

Our country's national anthem, or song, called "The Star-Spangled Banner" is truly one of the world's greatest songs. The song's lyrics, or words, were written in 1814 by a man named Francis Scott Key. He was an American lawyer and poet. During the War of 1812, Key watched as the British attacked Fort McHenry in Baltimore, Maryland. But when the sun came up the next morning, the American flag was still flying proudly over Fort McHenry. This sight inspired Key to write the poem "The Star-Spangled Banner." Key set his poem to the tune of an English song called "To Anacreon in Heaven." The song grew popular and was even printed in a Baltimore newspaper. Then, in 1931, "The Star-Spangled Banner" became the United States national anthem.

Write *fact* or *opinion* after each statement from the reading.

1. The national anthem of the United States is called "The Star-Spangled Banner." _____

2. It is truly one of the world's greatest songs. _____

3. The song's lyrics, or words, were written in 1814 by a man named Francis Scott Key. _____

Bridging the Gap

How to Train a Dolphin

1. Start by saying or showing a command, such as "jump!"

2. If the dolphin performs the command, use a "bridge." A bridge is either a whistle or a word, such as "good!" that you say right when the dolphin does what you want. If the dolphin does not perform the command, begin again.

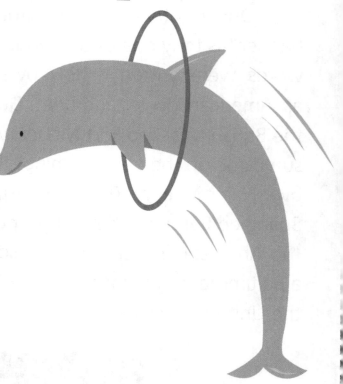

3. After the dolphin performs the command correctly, give the dolphin a reward, such as a fish.

Use the instructions to fill in the blanks.

1. Start by saying or showing a _____.

2. If the dolphin performs the command, use a

_____.

3. If the _____ does not perform the command, begin again.

4. Give the dolphin a _____, such as a fish.

Dolphin Detectives

Dolphins are like underwater detectives! They can locate things deep in the ocean very quickly. This has been useful to the United States Navy, which has used them to find underwater bombs.

Dolphins use sonar, or sound waves, to locate objects. A special structure on top of their heads, called a melon, sends out a beat of sound called a click. The click hits an object under the water. Then the object echoes, or repeats, the sound by bouncing it back to the dolphin.

As a dolphin gets closer to an object, the clicks return faster. That means there are more echoes. The echoes form patterns. Dolphins are able to form pictures in their heads with the echo patterns made by an object. Brilliant!

Answer the questions about the reading.

1. What do dolphins use sonar to do? Circle the answer in the reading.

2. What is a click? Circle the answer in the reading.

3. What does *echo* mean? Circle the answer in the reading.

4. What happens as a dolphin gets closer to an object under the water? Circle the answer in the reading.

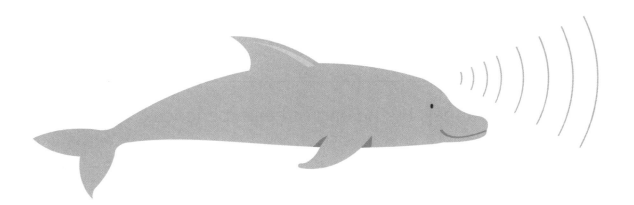

Dolphin Darling

Eva stood next to the dolphin pool waiting for the dolphin trainer. She was wearing a life preserver and goggles. She liked to look at pictures of dolphins and watch them on television, but in person the dolphins looked huge!

The dolphin trainer blew her whistle and two dolphins sped toward Eva. Her eyes grew wide. The dolphin trainer told Eva that the dolphins wanted to give her a kiss. Eva slowly approached the side of the pool and knelt down, as the trainer showed her what to do. Each dolphin rested its mouth on Eva's cheek!

Then the dolphin trainer told Eva to enter the dolphin pool. Eva shook her head, but the trainer urged Eva into the water. Eva swam to the center of the pool and waited. Before she knew it, the dolphins were on each side of her. Eva grabbed a fin in each hand and held on tight. They took her for the ride of her life!

Answer the questions about the story.

1. How does Eva feel at the beginning of her experience?

_____

2. What things does Eva do with the dolphins?

_____

_____

3. How do you think Eva feels by the end of her experience?

_____

Blue Ribbon

Callie sat up with her legs gripping Elmo. She held on tight to his reins and they circled the ring once more. A bead of sweat dripped from under her velvet helmet. She and Elmo approached the jump. She kept her eyes straight ahead as her chestnut brown horse leaped over it. Callie breathed a sigh of relief. It was the last jump of the competition. Callie thought they had done well. She worried a little bit about the third jump, but she hoped the judges wouldn't take away too many points.

Callie slid off her beloved horse and brushed his neck. She nuzzled her cheek against his and whispered, "Good job, buddy." Callie led Elmo to the edge of the ring, where her parents stood. At the same time they said, "You were perfect, sweetie!" Callie's parents always thought she was perfect, but right now she needed the judges to think so, too.

A voice boomed over the loudspeaker. This was it. Callie's hands became sweaty as she held Elmo's reins. The announcer called out the third-place winner, and then the second-place one. Finally, the announcer said, "And the blue ribbon goes to Callie West and her horse, Elmo." Callie threw her arms around Elmo. They had won the riding competition!

Answer the questions about the story. Write the letter of the answer on the line.

1. At the beginning of the story, Callie is _____.

   a. uncertain

   b. bored

   c. cold

2. How does Callie feel about Elmo? _____

   a. She thinks he's dumb.

   b. She loves him.

   c. She doesn't care about him.

Water, Water Everywhere

Oceans cover more than two-thirds of the surface of our planet. That's a lot of water! There are several oceans on earth: the Atlantic, the Pacific, the Indian, and the Arctic. Some scientists consider the waters near Antarctica to be a fifth ocean. Oceans are the largest bodies of water on our planet. Other, smaller areas of water on earth are called seas. These include the Mediterranean and Caribbean, in addition to many others.

One of the most interesting things about oceans is that there are actually mountains and volcanoes under the water! There are underwater ridges that form a mountain range nearly 40,000 miles long. These mountains weave through all the major oceans on the planet. In fact, the underwater mountains are the biggest feature on earth.

Ocean Facts
Area: about 139 million square miles (361 million square kilometers)
Average Depth: 12,450 feet (3,795 meters)
Deepest point: 36,201 feet (11,034 meters) in the Mariana Trench in the western Pacific Ocean
Largest ocean: Pacific Ocean, at 63.8 million square miles (165 square kilometers)

Use the reading and the chart to answer the questions.

1. How long is the chain of mountains in the ocean? _____

2. How much of the earth is covered by water? _____

3. How many square miles is the Pacific Ocean? _____

4. What is the average depth of the oceans in meters? _____

Crying Wolf

Read the beginning and end of this tale. Write your own middle part.

Day after day, the shepherd would cry to the local people, "Wolf! Wolf! A wolf is attacking my flock of sheep!" Everyone ran to his aid, but there was never any wolf and there was never any danger.

But one day, the wolf did come to attack the shepherd's flock. So, the shepherd cried to the local people once again, "Wolf! Wolf! A wolf is attacking my flock of sheep!"

_____

_____

_____

_____

_____

_____

You should not lie. You will not be believed when you are telling the truth!

Awards Accident

As I waited in my seat I was beginning to sweat. My satin evening gown was flowing around my feet. The huge diamond earrings I'd borrowed were weighing down my earlobes. I was running through my acceptance speech in my head. I had written it four times. I had to get it just right! The announcer began, "And the winner is..." Before I knew it, cameras were flashing all around me.

I didn't even hear whose name they had called, but I didn't need to. There was no question! The cameras were on me and the crowd in the auditorium was clapping loudly. I stood up, smiled, and waved. That's when the person next to me grabbed my wrist and pulled me toward him. He whispered, "You didn't win. She did!" He pointed to the nominee sitting directly in front of me. I slipped into my seat again with red cheeks.

Unscramble the words mentioned in the story.

1. minnoee _____

2. eescph _____

3. iwnnre _____

4. dautoirumi _____

Continental Divide

Continents are huge pieces of land on the surface of earth. In order of their size, the seven continents are: Asia, Africa, North America, South America, Antarctica, Europe, and Australia. However, some people think of Europe and Asia as one continent, called Eurasia, because they are connected to one another. Continents cover a little less than one-third of the surface of the planet, while water covers the other two-thirds.

Label the map with the names of each continent.
The labels have been started for you.

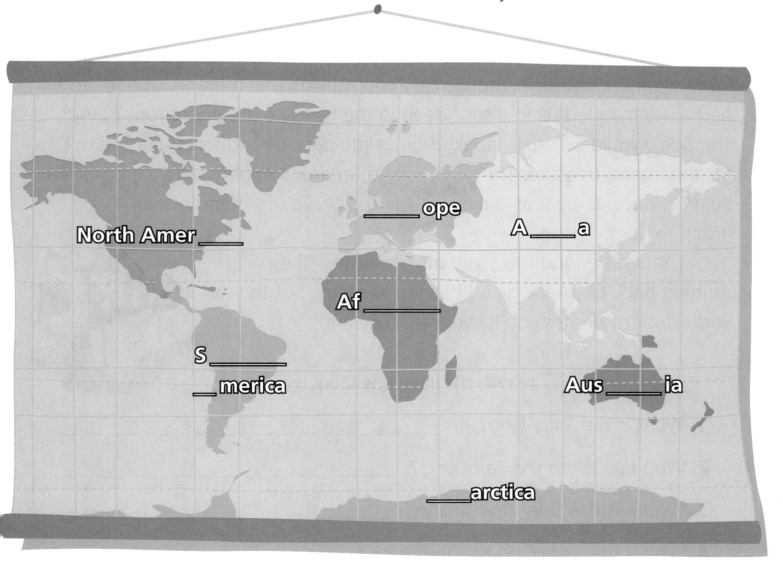

North Amer____

_____ope

A____a

Af_____

S_____
__merica

Aus____ia

____arctica

Pirates in a Panic

Have ye heard the tales of me ship, the *Salty Dog*? If not, listen closely. The *Salty Dog* was at port when we boarded her--me and me sea mates, that is. A pack of cutthroats we are, and proud of it! We cut her loose and set her a-sail in the waters of the Caribbean. The ship's captain was still aboard, so we shackled him like a beast down below deck. The *Dog's* hold was full up with spices, but it wasn't spices we were after. So we threw the sacks overboard to make room for what we hoped to get: gold!

Me mates and I set a course for a little-known island to the west. There it was said was booty for the taking. When the *Salty Dog* washed ashore on this island, we followed the map stolen right from the captain's pocket. Fool was still shackled below deck and couldn't put up much of a fight. He mumbled some nonsense about ghosts and then his chin fell to his neck. The map led us to a spot deep in the heart of the mysterious island. The gold would be ours! I looked on as me pack of cutthroats started to dig for the buried treasure. The wind picked up and a mighty blow came in. We heard a voice as clear as the eastern sun: "Leave this island at once!" it said.

That was enough to scare off me mates. They went running back to the *Dog* and pushed her back out to sea. Sorriest lot of pirates you'll ever see, they are.

Answer the questions about the story.

1. What is the *Salty Dog*? _____

2. Who has taken the *Salty Dog*? _____

3. Where is the *Salty Dog* headed? _____

4. Why is the *Salty Dog* headed there? _____

Caribbean Costume

Drew raced home from school this afternoon. Today was Halloween and he had to get dressed for trick-or-treating! He whipped open his closet door. Drew pulled out the costume he had secretly been making for weeks.

Drew slipped on black pants and a loose, white shirt with puffy sleeves. He pulled on tall, black leather boots and tucked his pant legs into them. Drew pulled a black eye patch over his head and placed it over his left eye. Next, Drew wrapped a red scarf around his head. On top, he placed a wide-brimmed black velvet hat marked with a skull and crossbones on the front. A long, white feather stuck out the top of the hat at an angle. As a final touch, Drew snapped a belt around his waist and dangled a toy sword from the belt. He glanced in the mirror and said, "Arrrrrgh!"

Draw a picture of Drew in his costume.
Label the picture with the name of the costume.

Solar System

Our solar system includes the sun and everything that revolves, or orbits, around it. The solar system is shaped like a flat disk. The sun sits at its center, and around it are eight major planets: Jupiter, Saturn, Earth, Mars, Venus, Neptune, Uranus, and Mercury.

The solar system includes dwarf planets, such as Pluto, which used to be considered a major planet. The solar system also has asteroids and comets, which are small chunks of ice, rock, and dust. There is also dust and gas floating around the solar system. The dust and gas was left when the solar system was formed.

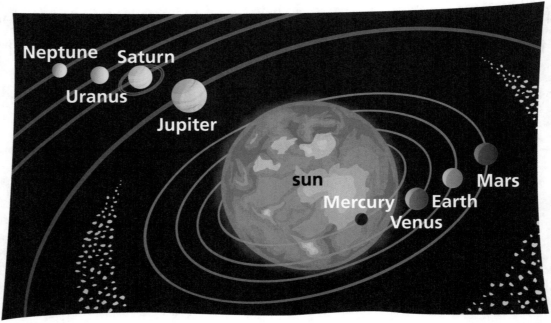

Use the reading and the diagram to answer the questions.

1. Which of the major planets is farthest from the sun?_____

2. Which of the major planets sits third closest to the sun?

_____

3. Which is closer to Earth, Venus or Saturn? _____

4. What else, besides planets, is in the solar system? _____

Dark Side of the Moon

The moon has no light of its own. The light that we see on the moon is actually light from the sun. The sun's light reflects off the surface of the moon. On some nights, the moon appears to be entirely lit up. But on other nights, Earth gets in the way. The Earth's shadow can block the light of the sun. On those nights, part of the moon appears to be dark. As the Earth moves, the round moon seems to change shape. When only parts of it are lit, the moon can look like a crescent roll or half a ball.

Draw pictures of the different shapes you have seen the moon take.

Sunny Days

The sun is the center of the solar system. It creates the light and heat we need to survive. All the planets revolve around it. But the sun is not a planet. The sun is actually a star! Like other stars, the sun is actually a bright ball of gas.

The sun sits about 93 million miles from Earth. It is the star closest to Earth. The sun may look small when you see it in the sky, but it is actually enormous. The sun is ten times wider than Jupiter, which is the largest planet. The sun is so big that more than one million planet Earths could fit inside it!

You should never look directly at the sun. The sun's brightness can actually hurt your eyes. To study the sun, scientists use special telescopes so they don't damage their eyesight.

Answer the questions about the reading.

1. What is the sun?

_____

2. What is one feature of the sun?

_____

3. How far away is the sun?

_____

4. What might happen if you looked straight at the sun?

_____

Suburban Spaceship

I was eating breakfast when I heard a strange noise outside. I ran to the window and saw a spaceship landing in my backyard!

The air outside was cold, so I threw on a jacket. When I opened the door, the fall leaves were blowing all around the huge spaceship. It was quite weird to see such a thing landing in the middle of my suburban neighborhood!

When I walked up to the spaceship, its doors slid open. A small purple creature greeted me with the question, "What year is it on earth?" I replied, "It's 2015." Then the doors of the ship slid closed and it sped away!

Fill in the chart to get a full understanding of this story's setting.

Year	
Weather	
Time of day	
Location	
Season	

Small Wonders

Stars are huge, bright balls of gas in space. You can see them in the sky at night. Of the different types of stars the most common type is called the red dwarf. But only a few of the stars that you actually see in the sky are red dwarfs. This is because these tiny stars give off less light than other stars. Red dwarfs are just too dull to be seen from the earth.

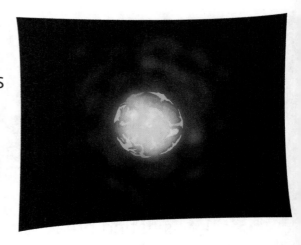

Red dwarf stars are small, and they burn very slowly. This enables them to live for a very long time. In fact, red dwarfs have been known to live for trillions of years before dying out. The slow burn of red dwarfs is what makes them red. Like fire, stars are hottest when they are burning white. If you look at a flame, its outer edges are reddish because that's the coolest part of the flame. Red dwarfs aren't as hot as many other stars, so their "flame" is red.

Write *true* or *false* after each statement about the reading.

1. Stars, like fire, are hottest when they are burning white.

_____

2. The fast burn of red dwarfs is also what makes them red.

_____

3. Red dwarf stars are the most common type of star out there.

_____

Hungry, Hungry Alien

When Keesha came down for dinner with her alien friend, Keesha's mother looked a little surprised. But Keesha seemed to like her new alien friend, so her mother made a lovely meal. The large, purple alien ate and ate until its little hands were covered in drippings.

In total, the alien ate two pounds of steak, one pound of green bean casserole, and one pound of corn bread. Keesha's mother looked at all the empty platters of food and raised her eyebrows. She said, "Well, I suppose I'll have to make another meal for your brothers and father." Keesha nodded. Her new alien friend sat back in his chair and belched. Then he said, "Great snacks. What's for dinner?"

Answer the questions about the story.

1. Describe Keesha's new friend.

_____

_____

2. How many pounds of food does Keesha's friend eat?

_____

3. Why will Keesha's mother have to make more food?

_____

4. What did Keesha's friend think of the food?

_____

Star Light, Star Bright

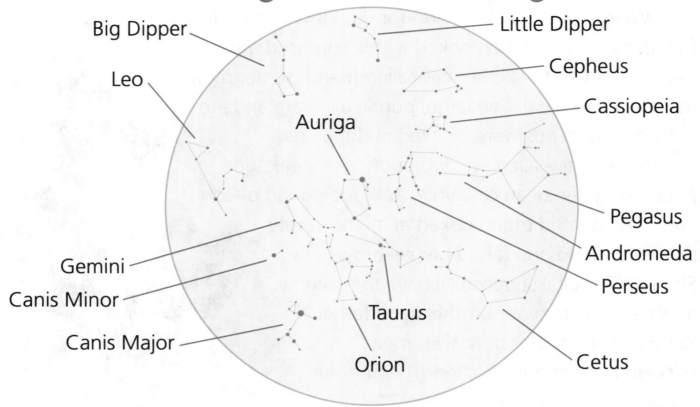

Big Dipper — Little Dipper — Cepheus — Cassiopeia — Leo — Auriga — Pegasus — Andromeda — Gemini — Perseus — Canis Minor — Taurus — Canis Major — Orion — Cetus

A constellation is a group of stars that are visible within a certain area of the night sky. As the earth turns, or orbits, around the sun, you can see different constellations. Not all the constellations can be seen at one time. During the course of the year, different ones become visible.

Use the reading and the map to answer the questions.

1. What is a constellation? _____

2. Do any of the constellations on this map sound or look familiar to you? Circle them.

3. Do any of the constellations on this map look or sound like animals? Circle them.

4. Which constellation is the farthest north on this constellation map?

Abby's Aliens

When Abby stepped onto the spaceship, she knew she was in for a weird night. The squishy yellow man spoke to her in another language and pointed to a seat. Abby obeyed and a thick belt bound itself tightly around her. *Uh-oh*, she thought, *am I a captive?* The spaceship shook and lifted off, which made Abby's stomach turn. Once they were in flight, the aliens began studying Abby.

One alien took off Abby's sneakers and socks and began smelling her feet. Another alien petted and played with Abby's hair. A third alien fiddled with the locket around her neck. Abby just sat still and hoped that they wouldn't hurt her. And they didn't, except for the alien that pulled a bit too hard on her hair. However, the aliens did leave Abby covered in squishy yellow slime. She looked like she had been sneezed on!

Complete each sentence about the reading. Circle the letter of the answer.

1. The main idea of this story is _____.

   a. She looked like she had been sneezed on!

   b. When Abby stepped onto the spaceship, she knew she was in for a weird night.

   c. One alien took off Abby's sneakers and socks and began smelling her feet.

2. The purpose of this story is to _____.

   a. persuade

   b. inform

   c. entertain

Space Race

Space Race is a term for the competition between the United States and the former Soviet Union to accomplish the most in space. The Space Race began in the 1950s when the Soviets launched the first orbiting object into space. It was called Sputnik 1. The Space Race continued when the Soviets sent the first man into space in 1961. His name was Yuri Gagarin and his spaceship was called Vostok 1. Just after that, the Americans sent a man into space, too. His name was Alan Shepard.

When the Space Race began, each side thought that space travel could help its military. At the time, the United States and Soviet Union were the two most powerful countries in the world, and they were enemies. This was called the Cold War. Each country wanted to be the best in space. Letting one country do better was considered shameful. So the Americans raced to get to the moon first. The Americans Neil Armstrong and Buzz Aldrin set foot on the surface of the moon in 1969. Their mission was called Apollo 11.

After the Cold War ended, the United States and Soviet Union spent less money on exploring space. The Space Race was no longer as important to each country.

Match each Space Race success to its astronaut.

landed on the moon	Yuri Gagarin
first man ever in space	Alan Shepard
first American man in space	Neil Armstrong and Buzz Aldrin

Spirit and Opportunity

Mars is the fourth planet from the sun. It is much smaller than Earth, and it is a reddish color. People have long wondered if there could be life on Mars. Recently, science has gotten closer to finding out. In 2004, two Mars exploration rovers called *Spirit* and *Opportunity* landed on Mars. They resemble large, remote-controlled cars. They are "driven" by scientists back on Earth. The rovers move slowly over the surface of the mysterious planet. They take photos, collect air samples, and test the natural elements, such as rocks, to see what they are made of.

So far the rovers have made one very important discovery: There may have been water on Mars a long time ago. This could mean that Mars is more similar to Earth than we thought. On Earth, where there is water, there are living things. So if there was water on Mars, maybe there was, or still is, life on another planet!

Answer the questions about the reading.

1. What are the Mars exploration rovers' names?

_____

2. What are the rovers doing on Mars?

_____

_____

3. What is the most important piece of information the rovers have found so far?

_____

4. What could this piece of information mean?

_____

Jumping Jupiter

Jupiter is the fifth planet from the sun. It is also the largest planet in our solar system. Jupiter is so huge that more than 1,000 planet Earths could fit inside it! Jupiter is not only larger than Earth. It also has a much different surface. Earth is solid, but Jupiter is a huge ball of gases. That is why it is often called the gas planet.

The center of Jupiter is hotter than the outside layers. Scientists think its center could be as hot as 45,000 degrees Fahrenheit! Jupiter and Earth do have something in common, though. They both have moons. Earth has the moon that you see when you look at the night sky. But Jupiter has more than 60 moons!

Match each number to its description from the reading.

1,000	**lowest number of moons that Jupiter has**
45,000	**number of planet Earths that could fit inside Jupiter**
60	**temperature of center of Jupiter**

How Old Are You Now?

One year on Earth is different from a year on another planet. You may know that one year on a planet is the length of time the planet needs to orbit the sun. The farther a planet is from the sun, the longer it takes to orbit the sun, and the longer its year will be.

Using the chart below and a calculator, figure out how old you are on a different planet. First, type your age. Then type the ÷ symbol. Next type the number of Earth years for another planet. Then hit the = symbol. That's your age on that planet!

Mercury	0.241 Earth years
Venus	0.616 Earth years
Earth	1.0 Earth year
Mars	1.88 Earth years
Jupiter	11.9 Earth years
Saturn	29.5 Earth years
Uranus	84.0 Earth years
Neptune	164.8 Earth years

Use the reading and the chart to answer the questions.

1. How old are you on Venus? _____

2. How old will you be on Mars after your next birthday? _____

3. Figure out how old your friends and family are on Neptune!

_____

_____

Grand Canyon

Jessica pouted for the entire car ride. She couldn't believe that her parents were wasting the family vacation on the Grand Canyon. Jessica was prepared for the most boring family vacation ever. First, Jessica's family visited the Tusayan Ruin and Museum and learned about the Pueblo Indians. Then, Jessica and her family went to the Yavapai Observation Station to understand how the Grand Canyon formed.

Next, Jessica's parents set up their campsite. It was nearly dark and Jessica was exhausted. The trip wasn't so bad so far. When Jessica awoke and zipped her tent open, she saw ridges and peaks in rusty oranges. The sun was rising and Jessica was overcome by the size of the Grand Canyon. Jessica and her parents went for a hike after breakfast. Jessica squealed

each time she saw a new animal. She even saw a condor chick! By the end of the second day, Jessica was convinced. "Can we come back next year and hike the other side of the canyon?" she begged her parents.

Find these words from the story in the word puzzle below.

hike   **Grand Canyon**   **Pueblo**   **Tusayan Ruin**   **condor**

H	G	R	A	N	D	C	A	N	Y	O	N
E	S	E	I	F	B	C	W	I	Y	K	Z
A	H	D	Q	S	X	C	A	E	N	M	T
L	P	U	Z	C	T	O	N	Q	H	A	U
T	U	S	A	Y	A	N	R	U	I	N	S
H	E	X	Q	E	T	D	R	S	K	Q	U
E	B	A	Y	N	U	O	F	Y	E	T	U
A	L	O	U	C	S	R	T	E	A	I	N
O	O	M	U	E	W	G	U	Y	T	N	V

Snorkel Trip

The boat stopped near the coral reef. Vivian pulled her goggles over her eyes. She held her nose and jumped from the boat's edge into the ocean. Vivian placed her snorkel inside her mouth, put her face in the water, and began to swim toward the reef. As Vivian swam closer, she was careful not to get too close to the reef's sharp edges.

The reef's wonders were a rainbow of colors. The reef was a peachy-pink color. To the left, a yellow and black fish darted by. To the right, green sea plants waved their hands at Vivian. Right below, Vivian spotted another fish. This one was shiny and silver. Then Vivian took a deep breath and dived down even closer to the coral reef. She needed a better look at the magical habitat. She came nose-to-nose with a flat, gray-and-brown stingray, which paid her no attention. The world beneath the surface of the water was a beautiful display of nature.

Answer the questions about the story.

1. Why does Vivian have to be careful not to get too close to the coral?

_____

2. Describe the fish Vivian sees.

_____

3. Describe the stingray Vivian spots.

_____

4. Why does Vivian dive deeper under the water?

_____

Weather Forecast

Weather is what happens in the lowest level of the air that surrounds earth. This blanket of air is called the atmosphere. Scientists describe the weather by measuring four things: visibility (how far we can see), temperature, wind, and precipitation (such as rain, hail, and snow). Weather is measured with tools, such as thermometers, barometers, and rain gauges.

Weather can vary from day to day, and that makes weather very different from climate. Climate is the average weather of a place during a long period of time. Scientists who study climates analyze daily, monthly, and yearly patterns of weather. Then they can describe the climate of a place.

Use what you learned from the reading to fill in the blanks.

1. Weather can _____ from day to day.

2. Climate is the _____ weather of a place during a long period of time.

3. Weather is what happens in the lowest level of the air that surrounds _____. This blanket of air is called the _____.

Winter Wonderland

The flakes fell furiously all night long. We stayed up late and watched them shine in the streetlights. When we woke for school, the windowsills were caked with luminous crystals. The roads were filled with the white fluff. Walking was nearly impossible.

We watched the television news closely. Our eyes followed the words going along the bottom of the screen. The closings were always listed alphabetically. As the M's, N's, and O's went by, our eyes grew wider. Then the P's darted across the screen. We let out a holler so loud that we woke the baby! We ran to the window once again to thank the skies for its white gift.

Answer the questions about the story.

1. What is the weather like in this story?

_____

2. What do you think the characters are hoping will happen?

_____

3. How do you think they feel about what has happened?

_____

4. What do you think the word *luminous* in paragraph 1 means? Circle the answer.

shining   dull   slimy

Winter White

A blizzard is really just a snowstorm. But it's a really bad snowstorm! The National Weather Service calls a storm a blizzard if two things happen for more than three hours. There must be winds of at least 35 miles per hour and visibility of less than $\frac{1}{4}$ mile. Blizzards usually drop fresh snow on the ground, but they also blow around snow that has already fallen.

As the wind whips old and new snow around, you can't see well. Sometimes the only thing you can see clearly is the snow. These are "whiteout" conditions. Then blizzards make snow drift up into massive piles. It is difficult to dig out after the storm has ended. Also, the air temperature during a blizzard is often below 20° F. This freezes water pipes and damages power lines.

Unscramble the words mentioned in the reading.

1. wheoutit _____

2. vbistyiili _____

3. nswo _____

4. frzeee _____

5. dnwi _____

Pete's Problem

Pete jumped off the ski lift at the top of the mountain. He skied forward to make room for the next people getting off the lift. Pete looked around at the peaks. His breath was white in the cold air.

Pete pulled his goggles down over his eyes, yanked his hat down to cover the bottoms of his ears, slid his hands through the loops on his poles, and set off down the mountain. Air rushed against his skin. It was cold and energizing. Tiny flecks of ice stung his face before melting. Out of the corner of his eye, Pete spotted another skier who had fallen down. She was right near the edge of the slope. If he stopped now, he would lose all his speed through the end of the trail.

Answer the questions about the story.

1. What is Pete's conflict, or problem, in this story?

_____

_____

2. What do you think Pete will do next?

_____

_____

3. If you were in Pete's situation, what would you do?

_____

_____

Snowball Fight

Danielle heard tapping at her window. A face appeared. Danielle's best friend Shannon called through the glass. "Come out! There's a huge neighborhood snowball fight!" Danielle slammed her math book shut and ran to the window. There was a blanket of fresh snow with footprints a few inches deep. She saw her friend Shannon running back into the rumble. Jack from next door was ducking behind a snowdrift. He threw a ball of frost at Shannon's back. Shannon then slid behind a tree and began making snowballs. She would have her own stock of icy weapons.

Danielle also saw her brother, Liam, stooped next to a car. He also had a pile of snowballs in front of him and was busy making more. Just then, his friend Kevin sailed a snowball in Liam's direction. It landed right on Liam's head! Liam shook his head to get the snow off.

Danielle knew it wouldn't be long before the boys ganged up against Shannon. She quickly slipped on her parka and snow boots, grabbed her mittens, and ran outside to join the battle.

Draw the scene that Danielle sees.

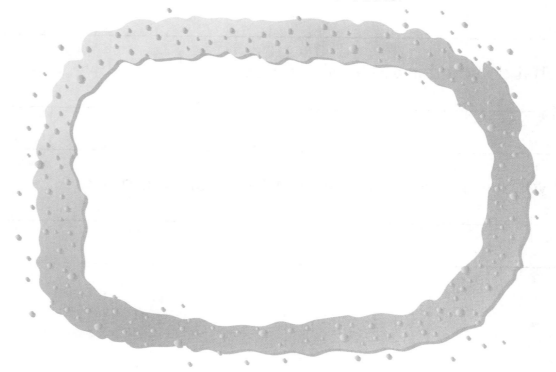

Let It Snow

A farmer from Vermont named Wilson Bentley discovered a lot about snowflakes. Bentley photographed thousands of snowflakes with a combination of a microscope and a camera. He was the person who discovered that no two snowflakes are exactly alike.

There are many kinds of snowflakes. Their appearance depends on the conditions in their clouds. Some snowflakes are simple and six sided. Others are more like tiny needles. The most well-known form a snowflake can take is a lacy shape like a star, flower, or fern. These snowflakes are called dendrites.

A snowflake can also be a six-sided plate. This type of flake sometimes remains hanging in the atmosphere. They glitter in the sunshine and are often called diamond dust. Did you know that snowflakes can look like triangles if the temperature is about 28° F? The number of shapes and sizes of snowflakes is endless!

Answer the questions about the reading.

1. Who discovered that no two snowflakes are exactly alike? Circle the answer in the reading.

2. What does a dendrite snowflake look like? Circle the answer in the reading.

3. At what temperature can snowflakes appear like triangles? Circle the answer in the reading.

4. What is the term for snowflakes that hang in the atmosphere? Circle the answer in the reading.

One Night...

Write your own beginning to this story.

_____

_____

_____

_____

_____

_____

_____

_____

The three trapped passengers wearily pulled themselves from the snow-covered car. It had been the longest night of their lives.

A Terrifying Tornado

It was a warm June day in Kansas. The weather forecaster said that winds were bringing warm, humid air in from one direction and cold, dry air from the opposite direction. He also said that these streams of air would meet in a low-pressure area. That meant one thing to us: tornado.

We heard it moving in as clear and loud as a train approaching. We all scurried into the underground shelter. I slammed the door behind us and bolted it shut. I couldn't see the tornado from below the ground, but I knew what was going on up there. The twisting, screaming funnel was plowing through our town at speeds up to 300 miles per hour. It was destroying everything it touched. It was picking up cows, cars, and sheds along the way. All we could do was sit and wait. We just hoped the door of the shelter held tight.

Answer the questions about the story.

1. What causes a tornado? _____

_____

2. What is one possible effect of a tornado?

_____

3. How do you think the author feels while she waits in the storm shelter? _____

Eye of the Storm

A hurricane is a very harsh storm that forms over a warm ocean or sea. Hurricanes deliver hard rain and extremely high winds. The winds, flooding, and large waves can cause great damage and loss of human life. In fact, two of the greatest natural disasters in the history of the United States were hurricanes.

In 1900, a hurricane struck Galveston, Texas. This hurricane turned out to be the deadliest natural disaster in United States history, which means that it killed the most people. The most destructive natural disaster in U.S. history was also caused by a hurricane. In 2005, Hurricane Katrina battered the coasts of Louisiana, Mississippi, and Alabama. The damages made the hurricane the most costly one to ever hit our country.

Use the code below to write the secret message!

A = 1	B = 2	C = 3	D = 4	E = 5	F = 6	G = 7
H = 8	I = 9	J = 10	K = 11	L = 12	M = 13	N = 14
O = 15	P = 16	Q = 17	R = 18	S = 19	T = 20	U = 21
	V = 22	W = 23	X = 24	Y = 25	Z = 26	

___ ___ ___ ___ ___ ___ ___
14   1   20   21   18   1   12

___ ___ ___ ___ ___ ___ ___ ___
4   9   19   1   19   20   5   18

Some Like It Hot

A heat wave is a long period of unusually hot weather. Heat waves happen when very warm air stays over the same place for days or weeks. Normally, when air is warmed by the sun, it rises up into the atmosphere. Cooler air rushes underneath to take its place and air temperatures get lower. However, sometimes the warm air gets trapped for a long time. Temperatures rise to higher than normal and remain high.

High temperatures can combine with high humidity, or moisture in the air, to make hot weather seem even hotter. The government uses the heat index to tell how hot the air actually feels. The heat index factors in air temperature, humidity, and the amount of direct sunlight. The government warns the public when the heat index may reach 105°F to 110°F or higher for at least two days in a row. The extreme heat and humidity can cause health problems, especially for older and sick people. Also, the energy supply is drained when people use cooling systems to keep homes and businesses cool. This can cause a blackout, when there is no energy for lights or appliances.

Answer the questions about the reading.

1. What is the effect of warm air becoming trapped instead of being

replaced by cool air?_____

2. What is the effect of humidity?

_____

3. What causes the government to warn the public about the heat?

_____

4. What are two effects of extreme heat?

_____

The Great Flood

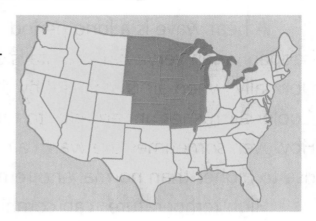

In 1993, heavy rain caused the Mississippi River, Missouri River, and other nearby rivers to overflow. The water in these rivers poured over their banks and across a vast area of the midwestern United States. This continued for several months. When the water finally settled down, 534 counties in nine midwestern states had been flooded. That area is as large as some of the Great Lakes! The results were terrible.

The event became known as the Great Flood of 1993 because it was so severe. It was recorded as one of the worst natural disasters in American history. Sadly, almost 50 people were killed and 55,000 homes were destroyed or damaged. Much of the Midwest was named a national disaster area. The damages caused by the flood totaled more than $10 billion.

Answer the questions about the reading.

1. What were two causes of the Great Flood?

_____

2. What were two effects of the Great Flood?

_____

3. Where did the Great Flood of 1993 take place?

_____

4. What does the word *severe* in paragraph 2 mean? Circle the answer.

bad   exciting   relaxing

Playtime for Toys

When the lights turn off and the house is silent, Jimmy the toy soldier makes his move. He hops off his shelf and begins waking the other toys. First, he rouses his army. "Reporting for duty, sir!" they respond. Then the army spreads out across the playroom. One soldier wakes the rocking horse and another soldier stirs the clown. Jimmy nudges the basket of stuffed animals until he hears the stuffed penguin chirp. The penguin waddles over to the teddy bear. The bear yawns and stretches his limbs to loosen up after a long day of sitting still.

The toys play the whole night. They chat with each other. Sometimes they play card games. But the last time the robot got a little loud when he lost a round, so they don't play cards much anymore. They can't run the risk of waking the people, after all.

Follow the directions. Use the picture.

1. Circle the rocking horse.

2. Circle the penguin.

3. Circle the toy soldier.

4. Underline the robot.

Opposite Day

Today is Opposite Day. That means everyone does and says the opposite of what they would normally do and say.

Use the clues to complete the crossword puzzle.
Remember that it is Opposite Day!

Across

1. dark

2. tall

3. bad

Down

4. slow

5. sharp

6. dry

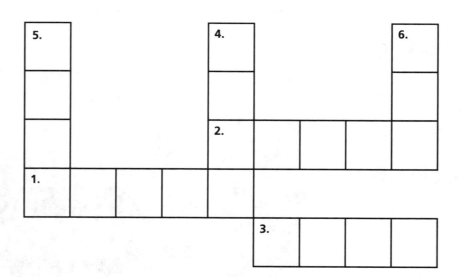

Ellis Island

In the shadow of the Statue of Liberty in New York Harbor lies Ellis Island, one of the most important places in the history of the United States. It was a gateway to this country for millions of immigrants, who are people who come to a country to live there forever.

Between 1892 and 1954, more than 12 million people passed through Ellis Island. They hoped to find a new, improved life for themselves in the United States of America. Many immigrants left the countries where they were poor and couldn't practice their religion freely.

After they passed some medical tests on Ellis Island, immigrants were allowed into the United States. Ferryboats took them into New York City, where many of them stayed to live. Many others traveled to other major cities such as Boston and Chicago.

Answer the questions about the reading.

1. Where is Ellis Island? _____

2. What is near Ellis Island? _____

3. How many immigrants passed through Ellis Island?_____

_____

4. Do you have any relatives who immigrated to America through Ellis Island?

_____

_____

Lady Liberty

We began a tour of Liberty Island in New York Harbor, just outside of New York City. We circled the base of the monument as our tour guide spoke. "The Statue of Liberty stands for freedom. It is a woman escaping the chains of tyranny, which lie at her feet. She is wearing flowing robes. The seven rays of her spiked crown stand for the seven seas and seven continents. Her right hand holds a torch that represents liberty. Her left hand holds a tablet with the date 'July 4, 1776' written on it. This is the day the United States declared its independence from Great Britain."

The tour guide asked, "Any questions for me?" I shot up my hand in the air and asked, "How tall is Lady Liberty?"

"She's 151 feet. With the base and pedestal, the entire monument stands at 305 feet. Thanks for coming today. Enjoy your time at Liberty Island!"

Draw a picture of the Statue of Liberty. Be certain to draw her robes, crown, torch, chains, and tablet. Include the date on the tablet. Label the statue's height, too.

Zoology Zack

Zoology Zack is a special scientist called a zoologist. "That's pronounced 'zoh,' like 'tow,'" he always says. "Zoh-ol-uh-jihst." Zack is my uncle. He is at Career Day at school to talk about his job. "Zoology is the branch of science that studies the animal kingdom, or kingdom Animalia," he explains. "The word *zoology* comes from the Greek word for 'knowledge of animals.' Modern zoologists study everything about animals, such as their behavior, the inner workings of their bodies, and how animals live in their habitats."

My friend Andrew raises his hand and asks, "Where do zoologists work? At the zoo?"

Uncle Zack pauses and then answers, "Well, yes. Some zoologists work at the zoo. But some zoologists work at natural history museums, safari parks, and other places where there are animals to observe and study. Other zoologists work at colleges and in laboratories." The class looks really interested. My uncle, Zoology Zack, has the coolest job ever!

Answer the questions about the story.

1. How do you pronounce the word *zoology*? _____

2. What is zoology? _____

3. What do you think Zack's nephew might want to be when he grows up? _____

4. Where do zoologists work? _____

_____

5. What are two things zoologists study?

_____

Water Cycle

Earth has a constant amount of water. But that water is always changing between solid and liquid and gas. How does it do this? Water changes form in a cycle. The water cycle has four parts:

Evaporation: The sun heats up bodies of water. The water turns into water vapor and goes into the air.

Condensation: Water vapor in the air gets cold and changes back into liquid. This forms clouds.

Precipitation: The clouds get heavy with water. The water falls back to the earth in the form of rain, hail, sleet, or snow.

Collection: Water is collected in oceans, rivers, and lakes.

Use the reading and the diagram to answer the questions.

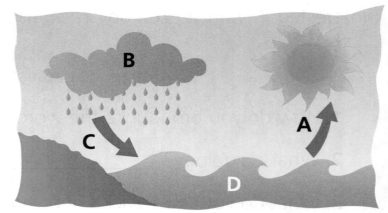

1. What part of the water cycle is happening in part A?

_____

2. What part of the water cycle is happening in part C?

_____

3. What is condensation? _____

_____

4. Which letter in the diagram represents collection? _____

Geography George

George adores geography. As his teacher describes places all over the world, he writes down her every word. Each time she unrolls the map above the chalkboard, George feels a tingle down his spine. When he goes home George closes his eyes and spins the globe in his room. He places a finger on it to stop it. Then he reads the name of the place where his finger landed and looks it up on his computer.

George can name the capital of every country and every state. He can tell you how long the Yangtze River is, where it begins, and what city lies closest to it. If you ask George about mountains, he will tell you about the highest peaks on earth. If you ask George about oceans, he will tell you the names of all the oceans and seas that exist. George thinks learning about all the places in the world is awesome. He can't wait to see them all in person!

Answer the questions about the story.

1. What do you think George might like to receive as a gift?

2. What do you think George might want to do for a career someday?

_____

3. How does George feel when his teacher opens the map?

_____

4. What do you think George wants to do during summer vacation?

_____

Michael's Magic

Michael Jordan is the best basketball player in history. He had the most exciting moves ever seen on a court. Even other basketball stars have said that Jordan was amazing. "There's Michael Jordan and then there is the rest of us," Magic Johnson once said.

Michael Jordan's basketball successes include being the NBA Most Valuable Player 5 times, NBA All-Star 14 times, as well as Rookie of the Year and Defensive Player of the Year. Jordan retired with the NBA's highest scoring average: 30.1 points per game. Michael Jordan was known for his amazing leaps and dunks.

1. What was the author of this story trying to accomplish? Write the letters of all the correct answers. _____

   a. give information   **b.** persuade the reader of something

   c. entertain the reader

Write *fact* or *opinion* after each statement from the reading.

2. He had the most exciting moves ever seen on a court. _____

3. Jordan retired with the NBA's highest scoring average: 30.1 points per game. _____

4. Michael Jordan is the best basketball player in history. _____

Hoop Dreams

A basketball is 30 inches in circumference. Circumference is the total distance around the outside of a round object. The ball is made from rubber or leather. It has a bumpy surface that is usually orange or brown. Basketballs are pumped full of air. They weigh between 20 and 22 ounces, depending on how much air is inside them.

In the game of basketball, you score points by getting the ball through the hoop. A basketball hoop has several parts. The rim of the hoop needs to be exactly 10 feet high. Its diameter, or width, is 18 inches. Basketball hoops have backboards attached to them. Backboards have a large rectangle painted on them. This rectangle helps players aim the ball into the hoop.

Answer the questions about the reading.

1. How high should a basketball rim be? _____

2. How large is a basketball? _____

3. What is the diameter of a basketball rim? _____

4. How much does a basketball weigh? _____

Field Day

Write your own ending to this story.

    As usual, Jonelle's name was the last one called. But she knew this would be the last Field Day when she was picked last. At the sound of the whistle, the race began. Jonelle bolted from the starting line. As she neared the end of her leg of the relay, she heard her teammates cry out, "Go, Jonelle, go!" After Jonelle tagged the next person on her relay team, she slowed down, looked around her, and smiled. She had run the fastest. Now her relay team was in the lead!

_____

_____

_____

_____

_____

_____

_____

_____

_____

_____

That Stings!

There are many types of creatures in the world that are poisonous. Their bite or sting can sometimes kill. Here are just a few:

The blue-ringed octopus is the most dangerous kind of octopus in the sea. It grabs its victims with its tentacles and then bites them. The saliva of the blue-ringed octopus contains a poison that is strong enough to kill a human being.

The king cobra is the longest poisonous snake in the world. King cobras have huge fangs that measure up to $\frac{1}{2}$-inch long. When it strikes, the snake's fangs dig into its victim. The fangs inject poison so strong that it kills creatures as large as elephants.

The Komodo dragon has a mouthful of trouble for its victims. The mouths of these creatures are full of disease-causing bacteria. When one bites, its victim gets sick and slowly dies of blood poisoning. After the victim dies, the Komodo returns to the scene of the crime to eat the body!

Answer the questions about the reading.

1. What is so dangerous about the blue-ringed octopus?

_____

2. How long are the fangs of a king cobra snake? _____

3. What does a Komodo dragon do after it has killed something?

_____

4. Do you think the bite of a king cobra would kill a human? Why or why not? _____

Nessie News

In Scotland, there is a lake called Loch Ness. In 1933, a new road was built along its shore. For the first time, the lake could be viewed clearly from its north side.

Later that year, a couple was driving down the new road. They spotted something very unusual in the lake: "an enormous animal rolling and plunging on the surface." Shortly after, the newspaper *Inverness Courier* ran a story about the couple's strange experience. The newspaper editor used the word *monster* to describe the animal in the lake.

Ever since, many stories of the Loch Ness monster have been heard and told. Hundreds of people claim to have seen the monster in Loch Ness. Some even think they've caught the mysterious creature on film. But there is no scientific proof that a Loch Ness monster truly exists. Even today, people continue to search for the legendary monster in the lake, who is affectionately called Nessie.

Answer the questions about the reading.

1. Where is Loch Ness? _____

2. When did the legend of the Loch Ness monster begin? _____

3. Who called the animal seen in the water a "monster"?

_____

4. What is the nickname for this creature? _____

Robot Ricky

Ricky had moved in next door a while ago. There was something my mom still didn't know about him. After visiting with Ricky's mom, my mom would complain, "Why don't you clean your room and speak politely like Ricky does?" I would just shake my head and reply, "Because I'm not a robot." "That's unkind to say," she would tell me.

One day my mom asked me to invite Ricky over for a swim. "That might not be such a good idea," I explained to her. "Don't be silly. Get that boy over here this minute and take a dip in the pool," my mom said. I shook my head again and called Ricky's house.

Ricky arrived with a towel and sunglasses in hand. My mom stepped out to the pool and asked, "Who wants to cool off?" Then she grabbed Ricky's hand and gently pushed him into the pool. "No!" I shouted. He fell right into the deep end! As soon as Ricky hit the water, sparks flew everywhere and I heard a weird buzzing noise. My mom looked concerned and confused. "I told you he was a robot, Mom. He can't get wet!" I pulled Ricky out of the pool and dried his circuits with a hair dryer. He'd be all right, but no thanks to my mom!

Use what you read in the story to fill in the blanks.

1. Ricky is actually a _____.

2. When Ricky went in the pool, _____ flew everywhere.

3. A _____ dries off Ricky after he gets wet.

Terrific Teachers

Teachers are people who help others learn things. For most of them, teaching is their profession, or job. Teachers usually work in a school, where there are groups of students. But teaching can also happen in a less formal place, such as at home.

Teachers pass on information and thinking skills to their students. They make a lesson plan for each new thing they teach. Good teachers consider the grade level, students' ages, skill levels, and whether or not any students have a learning disability.

Often, teachers' duties extend beyond the classroom. They are also responsible for taking students on field trips, organizing school events, and watching over extracurricular activities, such as music and sports. When their classes are over, teachers grade papers and projects, write report cards, and make tests. They meet with parents to talk about how their children are doing in school. In addition, teachers give extra help to students who are struggling in class.

Answer the questions about the reading. Circle the answer.

1. What does the word *extracurricular* in paragraph 3 mean?

     in school   in class   outside of school

2. What does the word *profession* in paragraph 1 mean?

     hobby   job   car

3. How might you describe someone who has a *disability*?

     less able to do something   expert at something   just okay at something

Good Sport

Use the pictures to answer the questions.

1. How does Max feel in the first scene?

_____

2. How does Max feel in the second scene?

_____

3. What might have happened between the two scenes?

_____

_____

Soccermania

Soccer is the world's most popular sport. It is played by people of all ages in about 200 countries. Soccer has millions of fans throughout the world. The sport is so popular that mobs of excited or angry fans sometimes charge the field.

There are a few reasons why soccer is so popular. It is easy to learn because it doesn't have too many rules. Soccer games are simple and inexpensive to start. All you need to play is a flat, open area and a ball.

An organization called FIFA governs all levels of soccer in all the countries that play it. Soccer is played by professionals, such as David Beckham, at the Olympic Games. The sport is also played in youth leagues. Soccer's biggest event is known as the World Cup. The World Cup is held every four years. During the competition, national teams from 32 countries compete against each other.

Soccer is the American and Canadian term for the game. Everywhere else in the world, soccer is called football. This can be confusing for those who think of football as a game in which you throw a pigskin ball around!

Answer the questions about the reading.

1. What is soccer called in most other countries? _____

2. Name a professional soccer player. _____

3. Why is soccer so popular? _____

4. What is FIFA? _____

Dentist Diaries

Sonia lay back in the dentist's chair. Her fingers were clasped tightly together. The dentist flashed a light in her face. She had to blink her eyes several times for her eyes to adjust. "This won't hurt a bit!" the dentist told her. He opened her jaw and approached her with a huge needle. Sonia felt a pinprick that made her flinch just a little. "Okay, the worst part is over!" the dentist tried to convince her. *A likely story,* Sonia thought.

Next, the dentist pulled out a drill and began moving it inside Sonia's mouth. She felt gentle pressure and smelled something burning, but she didn't sense any pain. A minute later, the dentist was bringing Sonia's chair upright. "All done!" the dentist told her. Sonia tried to speak "Un? Ow an ou ee un?" The dentist laughed. "Don't try to speak for a while, Sonia. Your mouth is still numb. But everything went well and your mouth shouldn't hurt at all later, either. You are free to go." Sonia walked out of the dentist's office with a sugar-free lollipop in hand. *That wasn't so bad,* she thought.

Answer the questions about the story.

1. How did Sonia feel when she first sat down in the dentist's chair?

_____

2. Did Sonia believe the dentist when he said that the worst was over?

_____

3. Why did Sonia's words sound funny when she tried to speak?

_____

4. How did Sonia feel when she left the dentist's office?

_____

Monkey Around

Harry ran over to the monkey exhibit. He pressed his face against the glass and tapped. "No tapping on the glass!" the zoo worker scolded. Harry frowned and pulled his hand away. Harry's parents were walking toward the door of the monkey house, but Harry lagged behind. They were too busy calming his baby sister to notice him. Harry ran to the door marked EMPLOYEES ONLY and pulled it open. He walked down a corridor and saw another door marked CAPUCHINS. He pulled that one open, too.

Soon Harry's parents realized that he was no longer by their side. They ran back into the monkey house. His mother shrieked, "We've lost our son! We've lost our son!" The zoo worker rushed toward them and said, "Don't worry! We'll find him. Everyone spread out!" The three adults began searching high and low in the monkey house. They looked in the bathrooms and by the entrance. That's when Harry's father shouted, "I think I found him!" Harry's father was pointing at the capuchin monkey window. Harry's mother and the zoo worker darted over to see. There was Harry, hanging from a branch on a tree, surrounded by monkeys!

Draw a picture of one scene from the story.

Fishy Lawyers

Lawyers are people whose jobs are to study the law and help people use it. But did you know that a lawyer is also a fish? Lawyer, mudfish, and dogfish are all nicknames for a bowfin fish. Bowfin are freshwater fish found in North American rivers, swamps, and lakes. A bowfin has a spotty, green body, a rounded snout with sharp teeth, and a long fin on its back. It feeds on other kinds of fish.

While human females are usually smaller than human males, the opposite is true for bowfin fish. The female bowfin is about 24 inches long and weighs about 12 pounds. The male bowfin is smaller. Male bowfins build a nest for their young and guard the baby fish after they hatch.

Answer the questions about the reading.

1. What is one definition of *lawyer*?

_____

2. What is a second definition of *lawyer*?

_____

3. What do bowfins eat?

_____

4. What is one difference between male and female bowfins?

_____

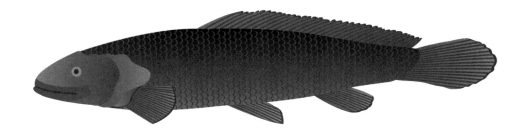

Little Red Riding Hood

Write your own middle part to this story.

There once was a girl named Little Red Riding Hood who wore a long red cape with a red hood. One day Little Red Riding Hood was skipping through the forest to bring a basket of muffins to her grandmother's house. That's when she crossed paths with a wolf.

_____

_____

_____

_____

_____

_____

_____

_____

_____

Then, Little Red Riding Hood, her grandmother, and the hunter left the wolf. All three of them were unharmed.

Lady with the Lamp

The most famous nurse in history is Florence Nightingale. She is known as the founder of modern nursing. Nursing was not always a respected job. Nurses were often not trained, so patients received poor care. But Florence Nightingale changed all that.

After the Crimean War broke out in 1854, Nightingale traveled overseas to the battlefields. She was very upset by the way injured soldiers were being cared for. Military hospitals didn't have many supplies. Also, the injured were unclean and diseases were spreading. Nightingale made changes, and more of the sick and the wounded soldiers got better instead of dying. Nightingale became a hero. She was called the Lady with the Lamp because even at night she would check on every patient while lighting her way with a lamp.

Because of Florence Nightingale's efforts, nursing became a respected medical career. Today nursing requires formal education and nurses have many important responsibilities. Nurses are a key part of the medical community, thanks to the Lady with the Lamp.

Use what you learned in the reading to fill in the blanks.

1. Florence Nightingale is the most famous _____ in history.

2. Florence Nightingale traveled to the battlefields of the _____ War to help improve the poor medical conditions.

3. Florence Nightingale checked on patients at night with a lamp, so she became known as the _____.

4. Thanks to _____, nurses are now a respected part of the medical community.

See Ya, Socks

"This is the last straw," Mark said. "Another batch of laundry, another sock is missing. Where are they all going?" "It's one of the great mysteries of life," Mark's mother replied. "You put two socks into the laundry and only one comes out. I think they are all having a party together somewhere." Mark wondered, *A sock party?*

The following week, Mark decided to solve the mystery of the missing socks. His plan was simple: he would watch the socks. Mark pulled off his white socks and dropped them into the washer. Then he bent to grab another wad of clothes for the load. But when he looked back into the washer, there was only one sock inside. *But how...* he thought, glancing around. And then he saw it.

A lone white sock was inching its way toward the door! Mark began to chase it, but the sock was faster than him. The sock slid under the front door, down the street, and into a clearing in the woods. Mark pushed

 through some bushes and finally had an answer to the sock mystery. In the middle of the clearing were hundreds and hundreds of socks! Some socks were eating chips and dip. Other socks were dancing. A few socks were even doing the limbo!

Answer the questions about the story.

1. What caused Mark to want to watch his socks?_____

_____

2. What was the effect of Mark acting out his plan? _____

_____

3. How do you think the socks decide which one of the pair will get to

escape? _____

Writing with Fire

Under each scene, write what the firefighter is doing.

_____	_____	_____

Bird Brains

Homing pigeons are birds with a very special ability: they always return to their homes. They can be brought anywhere and still find their way back to their pigeon cages, called lofts. Homing pigeons can fly more than 1,000 miles in just a couple of days, and they still return home to their lofts. That's why they are called *homi*ng pigeons!

There are many guesses why these pigeons can do this. Some scientists who study the way animals act, called animal behaviorists, feel that homing pigeons use earth's magnetic field to get home. But many other animal behaviorists think that homing pigeons are guided by the position of the sun. Still others believe that these amazing birds can identify and follow landmarks. The newest research on this mystery says that homing pigeons might be following smells!

Answer the questions about the reading.

1. Where do homing pigeons live?

_____

2. What special talent do homing pigeons have?

_____

3. What are three possible ways that homing pigeons do this?

_____

_____

Secret Son

Centuries ago, there lived a British king named Uther. King Uther had a son named Arthur, but no one in Uther's kingdom knew that Arthur existed. Arthur had been adopted by a man named Sir Ector. When King Uther died, the people of the kingdom demanded to know who the next high king of Britain would be.

Soon after, a mysterious stone appeared in a churchyard. Lodged in the stone was a sword with a message: Whoever could pull the sword out of the stone was the true high king of Britain. Many greedy people tried to loosen the sword from its place in the stone, but none were successful.

Years passed and the sword remained in the stone. Arthur had grown into a young man and one day found the sword in the stone. Arthur grabbed the sword's handle and pulled. The sword released itself from the stone! Arthur gave the sword to his brother Kay to use.

Sir Ector saw Kay's sword and asked, "Son, where did you get that sword?" Kay said, "Arthur brought it to me, Father." Sir Ector asked his adopted son, "Arthur, where did you get this sword?" Arthur replied, "I found it in a stone in a churchyard. It didn't look like it belonged to anyone." "Oh, but it does belong to someone. It belongs to the next true high king of Britain!" said Sir Ector.

Match the name of each character to his description in the story.

King Uther	adoptive father of Arthur
Sir Ector	adoptive brother of Arthur
Arthur	true father of Arthur
Kay	next high king

Bright Light

Write your own ending to this story.

Christopher and I were playing in his basement. It was dusty and smelled like moth balls. We were playing cops and robbers. I was the cop and had to find Christopher, who was hiding in the shadows of the basement. I could barely see, but I saw an old lamp on a table. I plugged the lamp into the wall. When the room lit up, Christopher and I were amazed at what was revealed.

_____

_____

_____

_____

_____

_____

_____

_____

_____

_____

_____

Football Fun

Peter looks forward to autumn Saturdays more than anything else. Every year Peter's father purchases tickets to the local college football games. Attending the games is a father-and-son tradition. Peter and his father take the trolley to the stadium. They wear the blue and orange colors of the local team. They meet with friends who are snacking and chatting in the parking lot.

Peter and his father find their seats inside the enormous stadium. The other seats quickly fill up with other fans. With the first whistle, the game begins! Peter and his father always cheer and wave their orange foam "fingers" high when their team scores a touchdown. Peter's father buys him hot cocoa at night games, when the air is cooler. After each game ends, Peter and his father board the trolley and head home. During the ride they talk about the most exciting plays of the game.

Answer the questions about the story.

1. How do Peter and his father travel to and from the football stadium?

_____

2. What are the football team's colors?

_____

3. What makes Peter and his father wave their foam "fingers" in the air?

_____

4. What do Peter and his father talk about on the way home after a game?

_____

Super Bowl Sunday

Each winter, the National Football League (NFL) season finishes with an intense game. The players are the champions of the American Football Conference (AFC) and the National Football Conference (NFC). The winner of this game, called the Super Bowl, is the NFL Champion that year.

Super Bowl Sunday is usually in January or February. It is one of the most popular sporting events of the year, so a lot of people watch it on TV. Companies fight for the chance to show their commercials during the game because so many people will be watching.

The Super Bowl also has a magnificent half-time celebration. Musicians, dancers, and other entertainers perform for the crowd. It is a great honor to be chosen to perform at the Super Bowl. Also, Super Bowl parties are a fun, popular activity that Sunday. Fans get together to watch the game, talk, and most important, eat plenty of snack food!

Write *F* or *O* next to each statement from the reading
to tell whether it is *fact* or *opinion*.

1. _____ Super Bowl parties are a fun, popular activity.

2. _____ The winner of this game, called the Super Bowl, is the NFL Champion that year.

3. _____ The Super Bowl also has a magnificent half-time celebration.

4. _____ Super Bowl Sunday is usually in January or February.

Amazing Alex

When I arrived at school today, my best friend, Alex, was waiting for me at the entrance. He said, "I have to show you something." Suddenly, Alex grabbed my arm and said, "I discovered that I have a special talent." Immediately my body became weightless. I looked around and saw that we were no longer standing on the ground. In fact, we were rising quickly above the flagpole outside Madison Elementary School!

"Apparently, I can fly!" Alex yelled out so that I could hear him over the roar of the wind. We were now moving fast and traveling over all the landmarks in town: the firehouse, the library, and the community pool. All I could do was hang on tight and take it all in.

When Alex brought us back down, we landed gently on the sidewalk in front of school. I felt a little sick to my stomach, but I managed to ask Alex, "So, what are you going to do now?" Alex smiled and winked at me. "I'm going to see the world."

Answer the questions about the story.

1. Why was Alex waiting for his friend outside of school?

_____

2. How did the author of the story feel after his trip?

_____

3. How do you think Alex feels about his special talent?

_____

4. What do you think Alex might do next?

_____

Declaring Independence

The Declaration of Independence is one of the most important and famous writings in our country's history. The Declaration was the official first step toward separating the original thirteen American colonies from the control of Great Britain. The Declaration of Independence also lists the basic rights that all American citizens should have.

The Declaration of Independence was not actually signed until August 2, 1776. But almost a month earlier, on July 4, 1776, the Declaration was formally accepted by the colonies. This is why we celebrate July 4 as Independence Day. On July 8, 1776, the Declaration was read to the public for the first time. The Liberty Bell rang to call citizens to come and hear.

The creators of the Declaration of Independence were John Adams, Benjamin Franklin, Robert Livingston, Thomas Jefferson, and Roger Sherman. The first draft of the document was written mostly by Thomas Jefferson.

Answer the questions about the reading.

1. How many American colonies were there? _____

2. Who wrote most of the first draft of the Declaration of Independence?

_____

3. On what date was the Declaration of Independence signed?

_____

4. On what day was the first public reading of the Declaration of Independence? _____

5. When is Independence Day celebrated? _____

Let Freedom Ring

The United States Liberty Bell is no ordinary bell. It plays a major role in history! The Liberty Bell rang on July 8, 1776, at the first public reading of the Declaration of Independence. Today, the Liberty Bell sits in Independence National Historical Park, which is in Philadelphia, Pennsylvania. But it took a long journey to get there!

During the Revolutionary War, British troops occupied Philadelphia. So in 1777, the bell was taken to Allentown, Pennsylvania. There it could be kept safe from harm. In 1778, the Liberty Bell was returned to Philadelphia and stayed in Independence Hall. From that point on, the Liberty Bell was rung on every Independence Day. It was also rung on state occasions. But then the bell moved again! In 1976, the Liberty Bell was moved to a glass dome near Independence Hall. Finally, in 2003, it was moved to its current home. That's one traveling bell!

Match each year to the Liberty Bell's location at that time.

2003	Allentown, Pennsylvania
1777	Independence National Historical Park
1778	glass dome near Independence Hall
1976	Independence Hall

Busy Betsy

Betsy Ross was a very busy girl. She had 16 brothers and sisters. She helped care for all of them. Betsy also did many of the household chores. In addition, she helped make clothes for the family of nineteen. All that sewing made Betsy a very good seamstress. Betsy continued to sew when she grew up. She earned money by sewing curtains, tablecloths, bedspreads, and clothes.

One day, George Washington came to Betsy's sewing shop and asked her to sew a flag. It was a big honor! Betsy Ross sewed a beautiful flag that was red, white, and blue. Her special flag became the very first American flag.

Answer the questions about the reading.

1. Why was Betsy Ross so busy? Give three examples.

_____

_____

_____

2. What tells you that Betsy Ross was good at sewing?

_____

3. Look at a modern American flag. How is it different from the flag pictured below?

_____

Billy Baseball

Billy knows everything about baseball, and he is a talented baseball player. He follows every team and every game on television and in the newspapers. He records all the scores, runs batted, players injured, and team trades. If you name it, Billy knows it!

Billy learned to play baseball from his father. When Billy was only three years old, he began to learn throwing, catching, and hitting. As Billy grew older, he became one of the best players around. The most amazing thing is that he can play almost every position on the field better than anyone else. Billy can pitch, hit, catch, play infield, play outfield, and even be a great umpire!

Answer the questions about the story.

1. What is the main idea of this story?

_____

_____

_____

2. What do you think Billy likes to do most in gym class?

_____

3. How do you think Billy's father feels about Billy's baseball talents?

_____

America's Pastime

As you read the passage, fill in each blank with any word from the correct part of speech. Have fun!

There is a reason it is called America's pastime: baseball is one of the most _____ and beloved sports in the country. People of all
ADJECTIVE

skill levels and ages _____ baseball, from Little League up to
VERB

_____ League Baseball.
ADJECTIVE

A baseball _____ is divided into nine innings. The team
NOUN

that scores the most runs by the end of the ninth inning is the

_____. Baseball innings have two halves. At the beginning of
NOUN

an inning, one team is at bat while the other is in the _____.
NOUN

Once the team at bat has received three outs, the teams switch places. For

the second half of the inning, the _____ team has a chance at
ADJECTIVE

bat.

A baseball play begins when the pitcher throws the ball toward the

_____, who is a player on the other team. The batter swings
NOUN

a _____ at the ball, trying to _____ it as far as
NOUN   VERB

possible into the baseball diamond. If the batter succeeds, he or she

_____ runs around a series
ADVERB

of bases. If a player reaches home base, a

_____ is scored. If a player is caught
NOUN

or tagged out before reaching home base, that

player cannot score a point.

Junk Drawer

The junk drawer is in the kitchen. It's the largest drawer in the cabinet. It needs to be big enough to hold all the little stuff in there! The junk drawer is a sea of things we didn't know we had, didn't know we needed, or didn't know what to do with. Some things in there even make us say, "I don't know what that is."

In the junk drawer are hair bands, toy soldiers, tacks, loose staples, tape, tweezers, twine, 22 batteries, a lime green padlock, a screwdriver, the lens from a pair of glasses, matches from France (we've never even been there!), flower food, rubber bands, loose change, coupons, candy wrappers, and fabric glue. There is even a strip of Velcro that must be part of a device somewhere in the house.

There are 17 keys in the junk drawer. We don't know what they open. There are 12 nuts and bolts in the junk drawer. We don't know what they should be attached to. There are four packages of half-used birthday candles in the junk drawer. We don't know why we keep buying more. There are 11 different buttons in the junk drawer. We don't know what shirts they belong to. The junk drawer is a collection of all the pieces of our lives that have nowhere else to go.

Circle all the items below that are in the junk drawer described in the story.

playing cards   collar   padlock   rubber band   pen

birthday candles   coupons   lip balm   watch   buttons

spoon   matches   sticky notes   tacks

Amanda the Avenger

Amanda slid on her gloves, threw open the window, and jumped. She soared up toward the bell tower at the center of town. As she flew, she watched the city below her. The grocer was stocking his shelves. The gas station attendant was working his pump. The school bus drivers were traveling their routes. But then Amanda spotted something unusual. She eyed a man with a black ski mask over his head. He was creeping along the outside wall of the bank.

Amanda slowed down and lowered herself to the ground in front of the bank. "What do you think you're doing?" she asked the man in the black mask. "Who wants to know?" the man barked back. Then he lunged at Amanda. But he didn't expect Amanda's reaction. With a kung-fu kick, Amanda knocked the man to the ground. Money flew out of his sweatshirt pockets and blew around the streets. "Just as I suspected," Amanda said. She picked up the man by the hood of his sweatshirt and flew toward the police station.

Answer the questions about the story.

1. What did Amanda see as she traveled over town?

_____

_____

2. What is Amanda's job?

_____

3. What do you think Amanda would have done if she had seen an old woman being mugged?

_____

_____

Thanks, Pilgrims!

On the fourth Thursday of November, my family celebrates Thanksgiving. My mom always wakes me up at 9:00 in the morning, just in time to watch the Thanksgiving Day parade on TV. The parade is in New York City, and it's the most magical parade in the world. Enormous floats travel down the streets and marching bands play. Santa Claus appears at the end. He calls the beginning of the holiday season.

All afternoon my mom is busy making dinner. The meal takes hours to prepare. But the result is worth her time and effort. There are mounds of moist stuffing, creamy mashed potatoes, juicy turkey, and sweet cranberry sauce. I top the turkey with my mom's super-secret-recipe gravy, which she makes only for Thanksgiving dinner. Before we eat, we hold hands and bow our heads. Then each of us says what we are thankful for in life. Dinner and parades are great, but giving thanks is definitely the most important part of Thanksgiving.

Using what you read in the story, draw a picture of Thanksgiving.
Give your drawing a title.

Explosive Earth

Volcanoes are places where hot gases and hot or melted rocks erupt through the surface of earth. The center of earth is extremely hot. That heat is always trying to escape out of the surface of the planet. When the heat rises, it also warms up and melts the rocky inside of the planet. This melted rock is called magma.

As magma moves toward the surface of the earth, it mixes with water in the ground. The water gets heated, too. It turns into a gas called steam. When this gas-filled magma reaches an opening in the earth's surface, it spews out. Once the magma has spewed out, it is called lava.

The most famous volcano in the United States is Mount Saint Helens in Washington State. In 1980, this volcano erupted and created a cloud of smoke and ash that was more than 15 miles high. The area near the volcano was destroyed and many people were killed.

Write *true* or *false* after each statement from the reading.

1. The center of earth is extremely hot. _____

2. Molten rock is called steam. _____

3. Mount Saint Helens erupted in 1980. _____

4. Where have you seen steam in your everyday life? _____

_____

Tommy and Marco

Tommy the tiger slowly prowled the jungle. His orange fur and black and white markings hid him as he got closer to his prey. Tommy the tiger crept toward the monkey, but Marco the monkey turned and stared at him. "What are you doing, Tommy?" Marco asked. "Who, me?" Tommy replied angelically. "Tommy, we both know we're friends, and so I'm off-limits," said Marco. "Come on, Marco, my wife's expecting a litter of cubs soon. I have to collect some food. And I can't let the other tigers know that we've made a deal. It will look bad. I'll look very un-tigerlike," Tommy protested.

Marco the monkey sighed and said, "Instead, why don't you roar and act scary before I run off? The other tigers will think you're fierce. How about that?" "Fine," replied Tommy the tiger before he let out a huge roar and stood up on his hind legs. His nine-foot body towered over the tiny monkey. Marco darted up a tree and whispered, "Same time and place tomorrow, Tommy?" The tiger sighed and mumbled, "Fine."

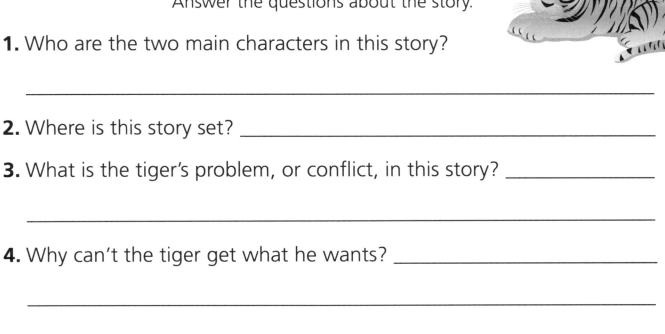

Answer the questions about the story.

1. Who are the two main characters in this story?

_____

2. Where is this story set? _____

3. What is the tiger's problem, or conflict, in this story? _____

_____

4. Why can't the tiger get what he wants? _____

_____

_____

 **Bright Ideas**

Thomas Edison wasn't the only person responsible for inventing the lightbulb. The English inventor Humphrey Davy had the same idea as Edison, but 70 years earlier! Davy created an "arc lamp" that was extremely powerful. But his lamp was too bright to be used in people's homes.

Next, an English chemist named Joseph Swan worked to improve Davy's arc lamp idea. Swan used a quick-burning carbon paper to conduct, or pass through, electricity. But Swan's carbon paper burned away too fast for the light to be useful.

Then, Thomas Edison took a turn at making a useful electric light source. Edison used a wire, called a filament, inside a glass bulb. The result was amazing. Electricity passed over the filament, causing it to glow and give off light that lasted a long time. Hence, the lightbulb was invented!

Answer the questions about the reading. Write the letter of the answer on the line.

1. What was the problem with using carbon paper as a conductor of electricity? _____
   a. It burned away too fast.
   b. It sucked up water.
   c. It didn't get hot enough.

2. What does the word *conduct* in paragraph 2 mean?

   _____
   a. to allow something to pass through
   b. to allow something to sleep
   c. to allow water to freeze

3. What was the problem with Davy's arc lamp? _____
   a. It was too dim.
   b. It was too bright.
   c. It was too small.

Marvin the Monster

Marvin lives in my closet, where he feels safe. But Mom is always trying to scare Marvin off. I don't have the faintest idea why. When I'm getting into bed each night, she asks me if there is still a monster in my closet. I always say yes, because it's true. Where else would he be? Then she asks if there are any monsters under my bed. It's a silly question, really. Marvin does not live under my bed. He lives *in my closet*.

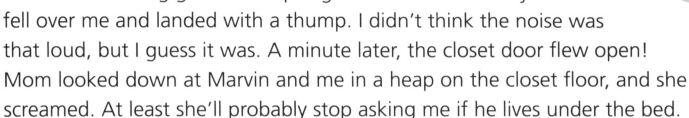

Marvin doesn't mean any harm, and he stays out of sight most of the time. But last night she saw him. After Mom turned off the lights and walked downstairs, I went into the closet to hang out with Marvin, like I do every night. It's the only time we can visit. Marvin and I had just started an exciting game of leapfrog when he accidentally fell over me and landed with a thump. I didn't think the noise was that loud, but I guess it was. A minute later, the closet door flew open! Mom looked down at Marvin and me in a heap on the closet floor, and she screamed. At least she'll probably stop asking me if he lives under the bed.

Answer the questions about the story.

1. Who is Marvin? _____

2. Where does Marvin live? _____

3. Why does Marvin live there? _____

4. Where does Marvin definitely not live? _____

Dino Dig

Dinosaurs were reptiles that first appeared on earth about 230 million years ago. Reptiles are vertebrates, which are animals with backbones. Reptiles also have scaly skin and lay eggs. But no one has ever seen a dinosaur alive. So, how do we know they existed? Fossils!

Special scientists, called paleontologists, study fossils. Fossils are the remains of a plant or animal that have been preserved in rock. After paleontologists discovered bones, eggs, and footprints in rock, they realized there had been creatures of the past that resembled gigantic reptiles!

In 1841, a British scientist named Richard Owen came up with a name for the long-dead lizards. He called them *dinosauria,* which means "terribly great lizard" in Greek.

Use what you learned from the reading to fill in the blanks.

1. A fossil is the remains of a plant or animal preserved in

_____.

2. _____ are the scientists who study fossils.

3. The word *preserved* in paragraph 2 means _____.

destroyed   **eaten**   **protected**

4. A _____ is a creature with a backbone.

Natural History

At the museum, Albert strayed away from his class. He wandered down halls and around corners until he came to a door marked DO NOT ENTER. Albert was never one to follow rules, so he opened the door and walked through. But instead of a private room, Albert found himself wading in a shallow lake. He looked around. *What on earth?* he thought. Albert walked out of the lake and began exploring his mysterious new surroundings.

After a few minutes, Albert heard a rumbling that got louder and louder. Eventually, the noise was so thunderous that the ground was shaking underneath him. That's when Albert came face-to-face with a huge Tyrannosaurus rex! Albert's eyes grew wide. He gulped and tried to forget what he knew about T. rexes. They're meat eaters!

Albert dashed back toward the lake. He held his breath, closed his eyes, and leaped. But instead of in water, Albert felt himself land on a hard surface. When he opened his eyes, Albert was sitting in a dark janitor's closet and dripping wet. *That'll teach me not to wander away from my field trip guide*, he thought.

Answer the questions about the story.

1. How do you think Albert felt when he saw the dinosaur? _____

_____

2. Why did Albert run from the Tyrannosaurus rex? Circle the answer in the story.

3. What is one thing you learn about Albert's personality? Underline the answer in the story.

4. What did Albert learn from his experience? _____

_____

Rubbed the Wrong Way

Andres was exploring the swamp near his house when he found a gold container that looked a bit like a teapot. *I know what these do*, he thought. Andres picked up the container and rubbed it. As he expected, a genie appeared.

"I am the genie of the lamp," the genie said. "Well, yes, that's obvious," replied Andres. "So, what are your three wishes?" asked the genie of the lamp. "Well, I'd like to win my baseball game on Saturday," began Andres. The genie cut him off. "That's your first wish? You want to win a game? You don't want to wish for world peace or a cure for all diseases or something else grand?"

Andres thought for a second and then asked, "Can you make those things come true?" The genie folded his arms over his chest and said, "No, but that's what people always wish for." "Well, if you can't make those wishes come true, what is the point of my wishing for them?" Andres asked.

The genie rolled his eyes. Andres continued, "Can you make me win my baseball game on Saturday?" The genie answered, "No." Andres knitted his eyebrows. "Can you make any wishes come true?" The genie said, "Well, no. I'm not a *magic* genie. I just needed some air. It's hot inside that lamp!"

Use the words from the word bank to fill in the blanks.

dialogue	author	characters

1. The genie is one of the story's _____.

2. When Andres speaks, his words are part of the story's

_____.

3. The person who wrote the story is called the _____.

A Tangled Web

A food web shows how living things depend on each other as a source of food. An arrow from a plant or animal points to what eats it.

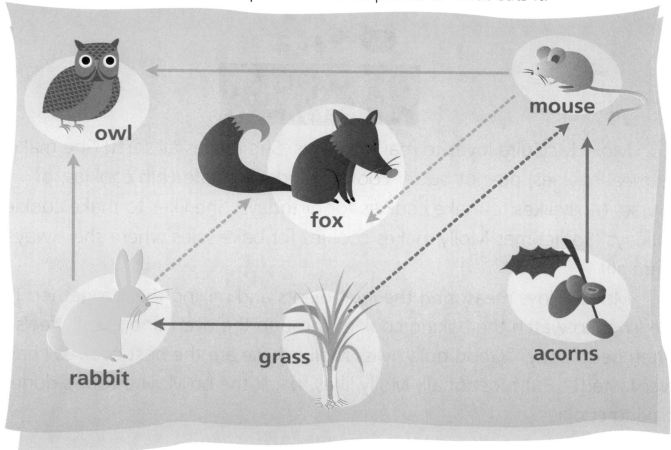

Use the food web to answer the questions.

1. Circle the member of the food web that eats acorns and grass.

2. Underline what the fox eats.

3. Does the rabbit ever get eaten? By which members of the food web?

_____

4. Draw a person on this food web. Add arrows to show what humans eat. Also add arrows to show if humans get eaten by anything on the food web.

Cookie Queen

Molly McGuire loves to make cookies. She makes all sorts! She makes oatmeal cookies, peanut butter cookies, and chocolate chip cookies, of course. Molly likes to make cookies for birthdays. She likes to make cookies for holidays. Sometimes Molly makes cookies for bake sales where she always sells them all!

Molly enjoys measuring the ingredients and mixing them together. Then she loves to watch the baking cookies through the oven door. Molly feels good when people say, "Good golly, Miss Molly, these are the best cookies I have ever tasted!" But most of all, Molly likes to lick the bowl when she's done making cookies.

Answer the questions about the story.

1. Who is the main character in this story? _____

2. What is the main idea? _____

3. Name three things Molly McGuire likes about making cookies.

_____

_____

4. What other foods might Molly McGuire enjoy making?

_____

Molly's Chocolate Chip Charmers

This is Molly McGuire's recipe for her amazing chocolate chip cookies. She calls them Chocolate Chip Charmers because they delight everyone! Ask an adult to help you make the cookies.

Ingredients:

1 stick of butter

1 cup of brown sugar

3 tablespoons of white sugar

3 teaspoons of vanilla

1 egg

2 tablespoons of milk

$\frac{1}{2}$ teaspoon of baking soda

$\frac{1}{2}$ teaspoon of baking powder

$\frac{1}{2}$ teaspoon of salt

$1\frac{3}{4}$ cups of flour

8 ounces of chocolate chips

Directions:

Preheat the oven to 375 degrees. Mix butter and sugar together. Beat in egg, vanilla, and milk. Combine the remaining dry ingredients in a separate bowl. Add the dry mixture to the butter mixture. Stir until it is dough. Place small balls of dough on a cookie sheet. Bake for 8 to 10 minutes.

Answer the questions about the recipe.

1. How did Molly's cookie recipe work? _____

2. Is there anything you could have done differently to make the cookies better? Explain. _____

_____

Cookie Culprit

The Quigley family was playing a board game in the living room. Mrs. Quigley excused herself to get a snack. The rest of the Quigleys talked and waited for Mrs. Quigley to return. Suddenly, they heard a gasp from the kitchen. "Who took the last cookie?" Mrs. Quigley cried. She walked back into the living room and every member of the Quigley family looked at one another. "Wasn't me!" they all shouted at the same time.

"A likely story," Mrs. Quigley replied, "but I think I can figure out who the Cookie Culprit is."

"Martin came home from school at 2 PM today. The last cookie was still in the jar. I returned home at 4 PM after picking up Jackie at school. The cookie was still in the jar. Dad came home from work while I was cooking supper at about 6 PM. The cookie was still in the jar. Since dinner, we've all been in the living room together. The cookie was left unattended in the kitchen." "So, what does that mean, Mom?" asked Jackie.

"Follow me," said Mrs. Quigley. The entire family followed Mrs. Quigley upstairs. She knocked on a bedroom door. A voice told her to come inside. There, Grandma Quigley sat in her rocker with a glass of milk in her hand.

Follow the directions. Use the picture.

1. Circle the family member who came home at 2 PM.

2. Draw a square around the family member who came home at 6 PM.

3. Underline the family members who came home at 4 PM.

4. Draw a star underneath the cookie culprit.

Qatar Questions

"Did you know there is a place in the world called Qatar?" I asked the class before I began my report. My teacher assigned us to do a report on any place in the world. I picked one I knew nothing about. I continued, "Qatar is officially called the State of Qatar and it's an Arab emirate. An emirate is a country run by an emir. Qatar is located on the Arabian Peninsula in the Middle East. The country of Saudi Arabia sits to the south of Qatar. Otherwise it is surrounded by the Persian Gulf."

James raised his hand and asked, "What's an emir?" I grumbled. James was always interrupting everyone. "An emir is like an Arab prince, or leader," I told James. "Both Arabic and English are spoken in Qatar and the currency is called the riyal. The area of Qatar is 4,247 square miles, and its population is only about 841,000 people. It's a pretty small place." James raised his hand again, "What is the capital of Qatar?" "The capital of Qatar is Doha. May I continue?" I asked. "The economy of Qatar depends on oil production. Like many other Middle Eastern countries, oil is..." James's hand shot up again. I don't care much for James.

Answer the questions about the story.

1. What is an emir? _____

2. What is the capital of Qatar? _____

3. Where is Qatar located? _____

4. What body of water borders Qatar? _____

5. Why doesn't the narrator like James? _____

_____

Poetry Puzzle

Bailey's Big Adventure

Daring to run
Out of the house, he
Goes dashing down the street!

Over the neighbor's fence, he jumps
Underneath their porch, and crawls
To dig up his favorite bone.

Answer the questions about the poem.

1. Highlight the first letter of each line. What do you notice about them?

_____

2. What do you think the dog's name is? _____

3. Write another three lines to tell what might happen next in the poem.

_____

_____

_____

My New Sneakers

My new sneakers are white canvas with a pink stripe down each side.
They have zippers instead of laces. That is the coolest part.
The zippers are what make them work.

My new sneakers are magic sneakers.
They make me run fast—faster than ever before.
It's all in the zippers.

My new sneakers make me run faster than a car.
They make me run faster than the wind.
They make me run faster than my brother!

My new sneakers are in the trash.
The zippers broke.
Now I have to wear my old ones with the regular laces.
It's okay. I'm still faster than my brother.

Answer the questions about the poem.

1. What do the author's sneakers look like?_____

2. What is special about the author's sneakers? _____

3. What happens to the new sneakers? _____

4. How do you think the author feels about what's happened to the sneakers? Explain. _____

_____

In My Tree House

Up in my tree house, I can be alone. It's quiet and there is no one to tell me to do chores or homework.

Up in my tree house, I can hear the birds chirping and watch them nesting. They are a soft blue and have golden beaks.

Up in my tree house, I can read a book and lose myself in its pages. I am the hero and the bad guy.

Up in my tree house, I can be anyone I choose. I am a sports star and supermodel who discovers a new galaxy.

Up in my tree house, I can see the world from above and understand it from this new angle. The world is a much smaller place from up here.

Answer the questions about the poem.

1. What are three things the author likes about being in a tree house?

_____

_____

2. What phrase repeats throughout the poem?

_____

3. Do you have a special place that makes you feel good? Explain.

_____

_____

Furry Friends

The Cheddar family lives in the basement of my building. They like the basement because everyone goes there to do laundry. Mrs. Cheddar tells me, "It's nice to have all those visitors." They have made a cozy little corner for themselves out of lone socks and old T-shirts.

All of the Cheddar kids are quite small and have gray skin. They look just like their mother. But Mr. Cheddar is a little pudgy and sort of brownish. He was complaining that he's out of shape. Last month I brought him an exercise wheel. He runs on it for 30 minutes a day, three times per week. "This will work off the cheese I've been eating all winter," he told me.

I told the Cheddars that I wanted to introduce them to my mom, and they were so excited! Mrs. Cheddar cleaned her corner of the basement and laid out a plate of cheese. The Cheddar kids took a swim in the washer so they would look presentable. When I brought my mom down to the basement, I led her over to the Cheddars' house, but she squealed and bolted back up the stairs! Some people have no manners.

Draw the Cheddars' home. Use as much detail as possible.

Made of Money

Money is anything that is used in exchange for items or services. The first coins were made in about 600 BCE in parts of India, China, and what is now Turkey. Hundreds of years passed before coins became the most common type of money used worldwide. The early coins were usually made of gold or silver. Their value was established by their weight.

Paper money began to replace coins for several reasons. First, new coins could be made only if there was a large enough supply of gold and silver. Paper money could be created whenever it was needed. Paper money was also lighter and easier for people to carry around.

Today, credit cards are widely used as payment. Credit cards work on a system of repayment. When someone hands a merchant a credit card, the merchant records the credit card number and buyer's name. The credit card provider pays the merchant for the good or service. Then the buyer pays back the card provider later on.

Write *true* or *false* next to each statement about the reading.

1. The first coins were made around 600 B.C.E. _____

2. Early coins were made of tin. _____

3. Paper money is easier for people to carry around. _____

4. Credit cards are commonly used in modern times. _____

Rome: Past and Present

A minute ago I found an ancient-looking coin on the ground. I picked it up and read the words on its surface: *Anno urbis conditae*. Suddenly I notice that I have on a draping robe and no shoes. A woman, dressed similarly, keeps uttering phrases to me in the same odd language that I read on the coin. I see a wax tablet in front of me with a pointed stick next to it. The woman keeps urging me to write with the stick. I decide to get out of there. I can't understand a word she is saying!

I walk outside and see an arena. We have those at home. I go to concerts there! Concerts are fun, so I head in to see who is performing. This arena is having a different sort of show, however. I spy a gladiator with a sword and shield. There is a lion hanging off his arm. The gladiator does not seem happy about that. Music sounds and someone named the emperor walks out onto a balcony. The crowd goes wild.

Back outside, I hear something drop at my feet. It's the coin! I pick it up again and repeat the words I read earlier that day. Before I know it I'm back home in Rome, New York, where there are no emperors or lions. But maybe that's a good thing. After all, there's no place like home!

Write *Y* next to the sentence if it describes something that, yes, happens in the story. Write *N* if, no, it does not.

1. The narrator finds himself in ancient Rome. _____

2. The narrator is at the circus. _____

3. The narrator sees a gladiator. _____

4. The narrator finds a magic coin. _____

5. The narrator eats breakfast with the Romans. _____

Unpaid Attention

"You see, class," Ms. Dupree explained, "a tadpole hatches from the frog egg and then..." She stopped. James was staring out the window. Madison was whispering to Julia. Conner was asleep on his desk. A puddle of drool dripped from his lips. *No one is paying any attention to this lesson on frogs,* she thought.

Ms. Dupree began to sweat. She wiped her forehead with her chalky hand. It left a smear of white across her face, which made the students point and laugh. She sighed. Then she walked right out of the room. The students looked at one another and then at the door. "Do you think the substitute is coming back?" Martin asked the rest of the class, "Or do you think we got rid of her for good?" The class shrugged. Just then, Ms. Dupree marched back into the classroom with a jar. She placed the jar on Conner's desk with a bang. He sat upright in his chair, with drool still hanging from his face.

The entire class stared at the jar with their mouths hanging open. "Is that a...a...dead frog?" Conner asked. "Yes, students, there is a frog in this jar. Cool, right?" Ms. Dupree said with authority. The students all shook their heads and still stared at the jar. *Now I've got them,* Ms. Dupree thought and smiled.

Answer the questions about the story.

1. What conflict, or problem, was Ms. Dupree having with the class?

_____

2. How do you think Ms. Dupree felt about this problem?

_____

3. What did Ms. Dupree do to solve her problem?

_____

A Frog's Life

Frogs go through a life cycle in stages. The female frog lays eggs in the water. There are sometimes 10,000 or more eggs! Inside each, a new life is forming. If the eggs are laid in a warm climate, they may hatch in as few as three days. But in colder weather, the eggs may take as long as 25 to 30 days to hatch. When they are ready, a tadpole hatches from each egg.

Tadpoles look like small fish. They have oval bodies with two small eyes. They have gills for breathing and a long tail for swimming. Tadpoles also have a tiny beak for scraping algae for food. The tadpole stage of a frog's life cycle can last just a few weeks or as many as three years. This depends on the type of frog. Most frogs spend about three months as tadpoles.

Then tadpoles grow legs and their tails begin to disappear. Next, gills are replaced with lungs, and their hearts, stomachs, and skeletons change. Their small beaks are no longer necessary. They grow long, sticky tongues that will help them catch insects. Now they are adult frogs!

Number the stages of a frog's life cycle in the correct order.

_____ Tadpoles grow legs and their tails begin to disappear.

_____ When the eggs are ready, a tadpole hatches from each.

_____ The female frog lays eggs in the water.

_____ Gills are replaced with lungs, and their hearts, stomachs, and skeletons change.

171

Some Major Religions

	Christianity	Islam	Judaism
Place of Origin	Israel	Arabia	Israel
Founder	Jesus of Nazareth	Muhammad	Abraham
Sacred Book	Holy Bible	Koran	Torah, Tanakh, Talmud
Holy Places	Jerusalem, Bethlehem, Nazareth, Rome	Mecca	Jerusalem
Major Festivals	Easter, Christmas, Lent, Advent	Id al-Adha, Hajj, Id al-Fitr, Ramadan, Milad un-Nabi, Lailat al-Qadr	Yom Kippur, Rosh Hashanah, Passover, Hanukkah
Main Branches	Orthodox, Protestant, Roman Catholic	Sunni, Shi'a, Sufi	Orthodox, Reform, Conservative
Sacred Buildings	Church	Mosque	Synagogue

Use the chart to answer the questions.

1. What are two similarities between Judaism and Christianity?

_____

_____

2. What religion uses the Koran as its sacred book?

_____

3. What religion celebrates Yom Kippur?

_____

4. Mecca is the holy place of which religion?

_____

Timely Gift

As Jeffrey approached his front porch, he saw a package with his name on it. There was no sender's name. Inside was a yellow bracelet and a note: *Wear this bracelet to see the world.* Jeffrey put it on and waited. Nothing happened.

Later that night, Jeffrey sat down to study for his science test. "I would rather be anywhere else than sitting here and studying," he said. "I wish I were at the beach." The very next second, Jeffrey found himself sitting on a white sand beach with a Mexican flag nearby. *What on earth?* Jeffrey thought. Then he looked down at his wrist. He was still wearing the mysterious bracelet. "It can't be," Jeffrey said under his breath. But, just to be certain, Jeffrey said, "I wish I were in London."

A second later, Jeffrey was standing in front of Buckingham Palace. Then Jeffrey said, "I wish I were in Africa!" Jeffrey found himself face-to-face with a lion! Jeffrey started to back away. "I wish I were back in my room!" he said with a shaky voice. Jeffrey sat back on his bed. He felt relieved to be safe from harm. He realized that power should be handled with care!

1. Match each location to what Jeffrey sees there.

Africa	**package**
porch	**white sand beach**
London	**lion**
Mexico	**Buckingham Palace**

2. If you could go anywhere in the world, where would you go? Explain.

_____

_____

_____

Olympic Games

The Olympic Games are a series of sporting events for athletes worldwide. The Olympic Games started in ancient Greece as long ago as 776 BCE. For hundreds of years, the Greeks held Olympic Games that included events such as wrestling, javelin, and running. The ancient Olympics were very competitive, and cheating became a problem. Also, emperors were demanding that prizes be awarded, which took the focus away from the sportsmanship. So they were banned in AD 393.

Much later, in 1896, the Games began again. That was the year of the first modern Olympics. They took place in Athens, Greece. The modern Olympic Games occur every four years. They are separated into Winter Games and Summer Games. The Winter Olympics consist of sports such as skiing, ice hockey, and bobsledding. The Summer Olympics include sports such as soccer, track and field, and swimming.

It is a great honor for each city that hosts an Olympic Games. Cities compete for the opportunity. Each one may launch a huge campaign to convince the Olympic Committee that it is the best place to hold the next Olympic Games.

Write *true* or *false* next to each statement about the reading.

1. This Olympic games started in ancient Rome. _____

2. This Olympic games were banned in 393 A.D. _____

3. This Olympic games occur every fours years. _____

4. Soccer is a sport included in the Winter Olympics. _____

X Games Xavier

This year's X Games are starting this week. I'm so excited to watch them! Tonight, the ESPN network aired a program about the history of the X Games. I learned a lot, such as the fact that the X Games are older than I am. The first X Games competition was held in June 1995 in Newport, Rhode Island. It featured skateboarding and BMX, but it was not nearly as exciting as today's X Games.

The X Games are often compared to the Olympics because the athletes are so talented and the competition is so fierce. Today, the X Games are split into Summer X Games and Winter X Games. In the summer, the Games include events such as motocross, skateboarding, freestyle BMX, and surfing. The Winter X Games are winter action sports such as skiing, snowboarding, and snowmobiling.

My all-time favorite X Games athlete is Tony Hawk, the skateboarder. He's not so young anymore, but he's still the best there is. I am always trying to copy his moves when I skateboard.

Answer the questions about the story.

1. When did the first X Games take place?

_____

2. What are the X Games compared to?

_____

3. What are three X Games sports?

_____

4. What do you learn about Xavier from the story?

_____

Presidential Pets

Pets have always been an important part of life in the White House, which is the house of the U.S. presidents. Thomas Jefferson had a mockingbird that hopped up the stairs alongside the president as he headed to bed. The Coolidges had a pet raccoon named Rebecca. John F. Kennedy's kids had a pony named Macaroni. Theodore Roosevelt, Jr., had a macaw!

For the most part, however, dogs and cats have been the pets at the White House. George Bush had a dog named Millie, and George W. Bush had his dogs, named Barney and Spot, patrolling the grounds. They also liked to fetch tennis balls.

When President Clinton was in office, his cat, Socks, crept around the halls of the famous home, too.

There have been so many pets living at the White House that there's even a pet handler who works there!

Answer the questions about the reading.

1. What do you think the responsibilities of the White House pet handler might be?

_____

2. Circle all the animals around the page that are mentioned in the reading.

3. Underline three Presidents named in the reading.

Grace Under Fire

Grace was curled up on the sofa, watching her favorite TV show, *The Life of the ER*. Her eyelids were starting to feel heavy. *I'll have to go up to bed when this is over*, she thought. During the next commercial, Grace went to the kitchen to get herself a glass of water. When she pushed through the swinging door, she saw people walking around. She saw cots, nurses, and many machines with lights and tubes. A doctor in a white lab coat rushed by her. He bellowed, "Get a move on, Grace. I need an IV in the patient in four, stat." Grace just stared at the doctor. Then she looked down and realized she was wearing blue cotton scrubs.

Suddenly, two doors swung open in front of her. Several paramedics pushed in a bed. On the bed was a woman who was about to have a baby. The paramedics looked at Grace. She couldn't take her eyes off the screaming pregnant woman. She stood in stunned silence. "Doctor," one of the paramedics said, "what would you like us to do with her?" Grace looked up at the paramedic and asked, "Me? You're asking ME? Why are you calling me 'doctor?' I'm not a doctor. I'm only eight years old!"

Answer the questions about the story.

1. Who is the main character in this story? _____

_____

2. What is the main character's conflict, or problem? _____

_____

_____

3. What do you think might happen next? _____

_____

Down to Earth

Think about how you drop a pencil, and it falls downward. You throw a ball up into the air, and it falls downward. You jump, and you fall downward. Do you notice a pattern here? Gravity is pulling all things down to earth. It will happen every time.

This invisible force called gravity even affects how tall you are. Do you think it's not true? Try this: Measure your exact height when you first wake up in the morning. Then right before bed, measure yourself again. You shrank about $\frac{1}{3}$ of an inch, right? Gravity has been pulling on your body. It makes you shorter over the course of the day!

There is a place where gravity doesn't exist, though: in space. Spaceships are far enough from earth that they are not affected by earth's gravity. Astronauts float in space because there is nothing to keep them down. Astronauts also stretch when they are in space. Without any gravity pulling their bodies downward, astronauts actually get taller while in space. Sometimes they grow more than two inches!

1. Perform the height experiment from the reading. Write down how much shorter you are at night.

_____

2. Hold this page up to a mirror to read the message!

ꓦꓤAVITY BRINGꙄ YOU DOWN TO EARTH

Write the message here:

_____

Mac Attack

Mark and Matthew were battling each other at Mac Attack, the newest video game. Matthew's character in the game wasn't performing the way he wanted. "If I were my character, I'd be zapping all the Macs much faster than he is!" Mark turned toward his brother to respond, but Matthew was gone. Mark looked around the room. Then he heard a tiny voice calling his name. Mark turned to the video game screen and squinted. "I'm in here! I'm in the game!" Matthew called out to his brother. "Help me! The Macs are attacking me!"

Mark quickly picked up his brother's video game controller and began pushing buttons. He had to save his brother! A green Mac jumped out of a pipe, so Mark threw a fireball at the creature. Then, Matthew found himself between two huge, blue Macs. Matthew screamed to his brother on the other side of the screen, "Quick, press the red and yellow buttons at the same time!" Mark followed his brother's instructions. But video-game Matthew turned into a puff of smoke and disappeared from the screen. "No! I killed him! I killed my brother!" Mark screamed in horror.

"Relax. I'm right here," Matthew said. He was seated next to Mark again and was a full-size human being. "Didn't I tell you about level 207 of the game? You can become a character." Mark just stared at his brother in disbelief.

Answer the questions about the story.

1. Why was Matthew frustrated with the video game?

_____

2. What became Matthew's big problem?

_____

_____

Chilly Chicks

Penguin babies are called chicks. Some penguin chicks stay in their burrow, or nest, for a while. There, their parents feed them. Other kinds of penguin chicks go to nurseries. These aren't like the nurseries where human babies are kept, though. Penguin babies are left alone while their parents hunt for food. But they have thousands of other penguin chicks in their nursery to keep them company.

When the parents of nursery penguins return with food, there is often a lot of confusion. The parents and chicks have to find each other among thousands of penguins. When the parent and chick finally meet, the parent penguin regurgitates, or spits up, food for the chick to eat.

When a penguin chick matures, the penguin swims in the ocean to find food. The penguin no longer depends on its parents.

Match each word from the reading to its definition.

matures   baby penguin

regurgitate   needs to survive

nursery   grows up

chick   large group of baby
                                           penguins left alone
depends
                                                       spits up

New Arrival

Today Shari's parents would be coming home from the hospital with Shari's new baby brother, Brian. Everyone was making such a big deal about Brian's arrival. Her aunt had decorated the house with balloons. Her grandparents had driven hours to be there. And her dad had even made a special dinner.

Shari tried to tell her dad about her science project, but he was too busy. Shari tried to ask her aunt if her outfit was nice, but Shari's aunt didn't hear her. Shari sat next to her grandpa, but he wasn't paying attention. Shari stormed off to her room.

An hour later, Shari's mom and dad brought her brother, Brian, home for the first time. While everyone else cheered, Shari pouted in the corner. Shari's mom brought Brian over to Shari. "Would you like to hold your baby brother, Shari?" Shari shrugged, but her mom placed the tiny baby in her arms, anyway.

Shari smelled his sweet baby smell and touched his soft skin. looked up at her with his dark blue eyes. Then, with his tiny hand, he reached for Shari's index finger and wrapped his fingers around it. Shari smiled and pulled her new baby brother closer.

Answer the questions about the story.

1. Why was today important for Shari's family? _____

_____

2. What have Shari's family members been doing to prepare for this day?

_____

3. How does Shari feel about this day at the beginning of the story?

_____

Lucky Day

Seamus spotted a tiny, bearded man dressed in a green suit and matching green hat. The man was no more than three inches tall. Seamus wasn't sure if he was seeing things. Then the tiny man spoke. "Okay, now you've seen me, lad. Shall I lead you to the pot of gold?" Seamus's mouth fell open. "Are...are...are you a leprechaun?" he asked. "Of course I'm a leprechaun! I don't wear this green outfit for the fun of it."

"Okay, then lead me to a pot of gold," Seamus told the pocket-sized person. "Follow me," the leprechaun told him. Seamus followed him out of the house and into the backyard. "Look there! The gold's at the end of that rainbow, lad." The leprechaun pointed at something in the sky. Seamus looked up, but he saw no rainbow. "Where?" he asked and looked back down where the leprechaun had been standing. The leprechaun had vanished!

The leprechaun ran off down the street, giggling "Silly lad didn't know the first rule about leprechauns. Never take your eyes off one, or it'll disappear!"

Answer the questions about the story.

1. What does the leprechaun offer to do for Seamus?

_____

2. How does the leprechaun distract Seamus?

_____

3. What is the first rule of dealing with leprechauns?

_____

Crocodile Confusion

Have you ever wondered what the difference is between a crocodile and an alligator? You're not alone. The easiest way to tell the difference is to compare their snouts. Crocodiles have a longer, more pointed snout, and their bottom teeth stick out a little. Alligators, on the other hand, have snouts that are broad, flat, and rounded. Also, you can't see the teeth of an alligator.

Crocodiles can be much larger than alligators. The largest crocodiles are in southeast Asia and northern Australia and can grow to be 28 feet long! The largest alligator ever found measured only about 19 feet long. While both types have been known to kill people (never go near one!), crocodiles are usually fiercer.

Answer the questions about the reading.

1. What should you do if you ever see a crocodile or alligator in the wild?

_____

2. Write the following words next to the pictures above to show which animal they describe.

crocodile	**alligator**	**pointed snout**
bottom teeth	**rounded snout**	**freshwater**
saltwater	**larger**	**smaller**

Cruising Together

The cruise ship had been at sea for three days when the sky began to get cloudy. Georgia and Thomas were on their honeymoon. They couldn't wait to reach the island. On the fourth day, the winds were whipping across the deck of the ship. And that night, the ship was rocking in the rough waves. Thomas felt sick to his stomach. Georgia went up on deck to see if the ship's doctor was there and could help her husband. That's when Georgia realized that the boat was sinking!

Answer the questions about the story.

1. What happened on the third day?

_____

2. On what day did the wind pick up?

_____

3. What do you think might happen next? Explain.

_____

_____

Grandma's Meatloaf

Jackie entered her grandparents' apartment building. The floor and walls were marble, which made the building feel cold and unwelcoming. Jackie watched the ancient elevator come down to the ground level. The elevator dinged and the doors slid open. Jackie and her father stepped inside. After the modern doors slid closed on their own, her father pulled the creaky metal door shut for extra safety. He hit the #3 button. The elevator began to rise.

On the third floor, Jackie and her father stepped out into another marble hallway. Jackie could hear sounds of life coming from each apartment. Jackie's shoes echoed against the floor as she and her father approached the door at the end of the hallway. Her father knocked lightly. Then he turned the knob. "Mom?" he called, before poking his head inside. "Come in, darlings!" Jackie's grandmother called back.

Jackie's father pushed the door open all the way. Jackie was immediately hit with the awful smell of her grandmother's meatloaf. Her father sighed and whispered, "Looks like she made her 'famous' dinner again, Jacs. Just smile and then feed it to the dog under the table, okay?" Jackie just smiled.

Answer the questions about the story.

1. What is one thing that Jackie sees in her grandparents' apartment building? _____

2. What is one thing that Jackie hears in the building?

   _____

3. Name something Jackie smells in her grandparents' apartment building.

   _____

Scary Sun

There is nothing healthy about a suntan or sunburn. When the ultraviolet, or UV, rays of the sun hit your skin, they damage your body. So when your skin changes color after being in the sun, your skin is actually telling you that it has been hurt!

There are many ways to protect yourself from the harmful UV rays of the sun. First, you should stay out of the sun as much as possible. When you are outdoors, be sure to wear protective clothing, such as a sun hat and sunglasses. Avoid the sun during its peak hours, which are between 10 AM and 2 PM. Also, always wear sunscreen with a high SPF number.

Sunscreens are special lotions that protect your bare skin from UV damage. SPF stands for Sun Protection Factor. SPF is marked with a number on the front of a sunscreen container. The SPF number indicates how much of the sun's rays will be blocked out by the lotion. Using an SPF of 15 or higher can decrease your risk of getting skin cancer by 78 percent.

1. Sometimes an author can have more than one reason for writing a story. Place a check next to all the reasons why you think the author wrote this story.

   _____ to convince people to protect themselves from the sun

   _____ to give information about the risks of the sun

   _____ to make the reader laugh about sun damage

2. What are three things you can do to protect yourself from the sun?

   _____

   _____

   _____

Moments in Time

Kerrie and Ted knelt on the ground by a fence. Each had a trowel, and they began to dig. Five years ago, the two friends had buried a time capsule. "We were only five when we buried this," began Ted, "so who knows what kinds of funny things we put inside it."

After a few minutes of shoveling up earth, Kerrie's trowel finally hit something hard. She tapped at it and heard an echo. "Jackpot!" she exclaimed. Ted lifted the box from the ground and pried open its lid.

The contents of the box were a coloring book and crayons, a blue ribbon from Ted's first swim meet, a trophy from Kerrie's first horseback-riding competition, and two letters. One letter was written by Kerrie and the other by Ted. In the letters, they had written their favorite things, as well as the things they hated the most at the age of five.

The two friends rolled on the ground, laughing at what they had written so long ago. Then they flipped over the pages and started to write. This time they were writing about themselves at age ten. They returned the letters to the box. Kerrie added her favorite silver ring from her finger. Ted took his lucky coin from his jeans pocket and tossed it in the box. They would be back in five years.

Answer the questions about the story.

1. What did Kerrie and Ted find in their time capsule?

_____

2. What do Kerrie and Ted add to their time capsule?

_____

3. How did Kerrie and Ted react to their time capsule?

_____

Answer Key

Page 6
1. garlic
2. Answers will vary.
3.

Page 7
1.

calf

2.

kitten

3.

puppy

4.

joey

Page 8
1. Zoey
2.

3. deserted island

Page 9
1. femur or thighbone
2. stapes
3. 300, 206

Page 10
1. 2009
2. 2109
3. cars of the future

Page 11
The following words should be circled:
1. Bluebird

2. New York City
3. Sugar maple
4. Statue of Liberty, National Baseball Hall of Fame and Museum

Page 12
1. basketball
2. bumblebee
3. banana

Page 13
1. _5_ The winner becomes "It" and a new round of Dibble Dabble begins.
_2_ "It" dives deep under the water and lets go of the stick.
_4_ Everyone jumps into the water, and the player who grabs the stick wins the game.
_3_ The other players watch the water.
_1_ All the players stand on the edge of the dock.

2. You must know how to swim well.

Page 14
1. English and French
2. hockey, beautiful landscapes, or cold weather
3. Ottawa
4. red and white

Page 15
1. author
2. summary
3. review
4. read

Page 16
Answers will vary.

Page 17
1. b
2. c
3. b

Page 18
1. no
2. yes
3. no
4. no

Page 19
1.

2. music star
3. Answers will vary.

Page 20
1. opinion
2. fact
3. opinion

Page 21
1. food, such as turkey
2. laughter, dog begging for food
3. glass, dog's head, utensils

Page 22
1. no
2. no
3. yes
4. no

Page 23
1. possible answers: sad, upset, embarrassed
2. Smith
3.

Page 24
1. to give information

2.
3.

Page 25
1. possible answers: He wasn't able to study for long. He had a hard time focusing on the test.
2. possible answers: Sam was grounded for a weekend. His parents were unhappy. He studied harder for the next test.

Page 26

¹f		²s	o	³c	c	e	r
⁴a	r	t		r			
m				a			
i				f			
l				t			
y		⁵s	w	i	m	m	i	n	g

Page 27
1. Pacific
2. equator
3. Andes
4. Galapagos

Page 28
1. b
2. b
3. c

Page 29
1. true
2. false
3. true

Page 30
Stories will vary.

Page 31
1.

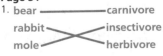

2. Mammals have warm blood, a backbone, fur or hair, and females that produce milk for their young.

Page 32
1. Jenny
2. John
3. possible answers: Jenny is trying to make an erupting volcano. Jenny is the first clarinet chair in band this year. Jenny has been practicing her clarinet a lot.
4. possible answers: John plays soccer. John played halfback last year.

Page 33
1. _2_ Add milk and blend until mixture is moist.
_1_ Mix flour, baking powder, and salt.
_4_ Bake on a greased pan at 475 degrees for 12 to 15 minutes.
_3_ Lightly knead the mixture on a surface sprinkled with flour.

2. The biscuits will be under-cooked.

Page 34
1. In the passage, circle "Just down the street, in the house with the white shutters, lives the Bird Lady."
2. Underline "What they do know is that the Bird Lady sits silent and still on her porch for hours every day. She sits so still that all the birds come and rest on her." and "But the Bird Lady never moves an inch."
3.

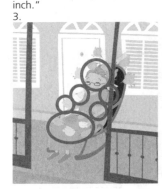

Page 35
1. military
2. World War I
3. Armistice

Page 36
1. The narrator is stuck in the middle of the backseat of a car.
2. He is unhappy and frustrated.
3. He complains about everything that makes him uncomfortable.
4. Answers will vary.

Page 37
first image matches Jack and Sam, second image matches Trevor and Adam, third image matches Jessie, fourth image matches Melvin

Page 38
1. Steel is much stronger than most other building materials.
2. possible answers: Empire State Building, Sears Tower
3. Because they are built upward.

Page 39
1. She slept in a sleeping bag on a cot. She walked to the mess hall for breakfast. She cleaned the mess hall. She cleaned the toilets.
2. A diva is someone who demands to be treated like a princess.
3. No, she didn't like all the work she had to do.

Page 40
<u>4</u> Oscar just purred and curled up next to Susan's pillow.
<u>2</u> Susan checked everywhere for Oscar.
<u>1</u> Susan hadn't seen Oscar for hours.
<u>3</u> When Susan went to bed that night, she felt worried and scared for Oscar.

Page 41
1. The following words should be circled in the story: tall trees and taller buildings, cars.
2. The following should be underlined in the passage: construction noises, traffic, and people talking.
3. The following words should be boxed in the passage: trash and car fumes.

Page 42
1. sun
2. spring
3. revolve
4. daylight
5. season

Page 43
1. Answers will vary.
2. possible answers: shave, drive, go to work, wear a tie, make dinner

Page 44
1. polar
2. yellow
3. shots

Page 45
1. possible answers: the weather, ice cream, the zoo, kittens, movies, hopscotch, cotton candy, the beach, bicycle rides
2. No, because she doesn't seem to like anything.
3. her friend, the narrator

Page 46
1. fact
2. fact
3. inform, persuade

Page 47
1. bogs, swamps, and marshes
2. They store water.
3. possible answers: killing wildlife, running out of water, dirty water

Page 48

Page 49
1. to inform readers and to persuade readers
2. 3 percent
3. pumping it

Page 50
There are many ways to conserve, or save, energy.

Page 51
1. eight
2. $2
3. $1
4. $8.50

Page 52

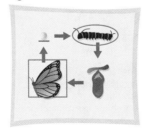

Page 53

Page 54
1. fact
2. opinion
3. opinion
4. fact

Page 55
1. Hello! How are you?
2. Excuse me, where are the bathrooms?

Page 56
1. Capitol Hill
2. September 18, 1793
3. William Thornton

4. possible answers: Rotunda, Senate Chamber, House Chamber, President's Room, National Statuary Hall

Page 57
<u>4</u> Place the tray carefully into the freezer.
<u>2</u> Tightly seal the entire tray with plastic wrap.
<u>3</u> Place one toothpick in the center of each cube by poking a hole through the plastic.
<u>1</u> Fill an empty ice cube tray with the juice.

Page 58
Answers will vary.

Page 59
1. hippocampus
2. Answers will vary.
3. Answers will vary.

Page 60
Answers will vary.

Page 61
<u>hiding</u>
<u>bark</u>
<u>tracking</u>
<u>smell</u>
<u>five</u>
<u>humans</u>

Page 62

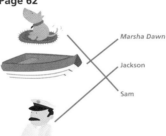

Page 63

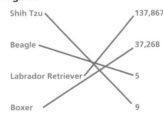

Page 64
1. dogs
2. a veterinarian or animal shelter worker
3. He would take care of it and find it a new home.
4. They probably love Mike.

Page 65
1. second picture
2. last picture
3. first picture

Page 66
1. Her puppy is not doing well in puppy school, so he may need to go to another home.
2. She doesn't want to lose her puppy. She will train him.

3. She practiced commands with her puppy every day.
4. Paula probably felt happy and proud.

Page 67
1. The following phrases should be circled:
"clears the dishes from the table," "returns the milk to the refrigerator," "sweeps up the crumbs under the table," "drops the used napkins in the hamper"
2. He doesn't like them.
3. His mom needs help with work around the house.
4. Answers will vary.

Page 68
1. puffy
2. looks like
3. surface

Page 69
1. true
2. true
3. false
4. true
5. false

Page 70
Drawings will vary.

Page 71
1. c
2. a
3. Answers will vary.

Page 72
Titles and stories will vary.

Page 73
1. head
2. carrying food, digging, defending themselves
3. climbing and clinging to things
4. metasoma

Page 74
Answers will vary.

Page 75
1. a
2. b
3. a
4. c

Page 76
Drawings will vary.

Page 77
1. five
2. Southwest
3. possible answers: Wampanoag, Iroquois, Narraganset, Delaware, Shawnee, Powhatan, Illinois, Cherokee, Creek, Chickasaw, Natchez, Timucuan

Page 78
<u>2</u> She calls her father into her room.
<u>4</u> After a half hour, he marks Claire's page in the book, kisses her goodnight, and switches off her bedside lamp.
<u>3</u> She props up her pillows and opens the book to where she left off.

_1_ After dinner and chores, Claire climbs the stairs to put on her pajamas, brush her teeth, and wash her face.

Page 79
1. fact
2. opinion
3. fact

Page 80
1. command
2. bridge
3. dolphin
4. reward

Page 81
The following should be circled in the passage: 1. "locate objects", 2. "beat of sound", 3. "repeats", 4. "the clicks are made more often," "Dolphins are able to form pictures in their heads with the echo patterns made by an object."

Page 82
1. Eva is scared.
2. Eva lets them kiss her, and then she rides with them.
3. Eva is glad that she did it.

Page 83
1. a
2. b

Page 84
1. 40,000 miles
2. two-thirds
3. 63.8 million
4. 3,795

Page 85
Stories will vary.

Page 86
1. nominee
2. speech
3. winner
4. auditorium

Page 87

Page 88
1. a ship
2. pirates
3. an island to the west
4. to find treasure, booty, gold

Page 89
Drawings will vary, but should include label "pirate."

Page 90
1. Neptune
2. Earth
3. Venus
4. possible answers: asteroids, comets, dust, gas, the sun

Page 91
Drawings will vary.

Page 92
1. a star
2. possible answers: it creates heat and light, it is a bright ball of gas, it is enormous
3. 93 million miles
4. You would damage your eyes.

Page 93

Year	2015
Weather	cold
Time of day	morning
Location	backyard in suburbs
Season	fall

Page 94
1. true
2. false
3. true

Page 95
1. Her friend is a large, purple alien with little hands.
2. four
3. The alien ate it all.
4. He said it was great.

Page 96
1. A constellation is a group of stars that are visible within a certain area of the night sky.
2. Answers will vary.
3. Answers will vary.
4. Little Dipper

Page 97
1. b
2. c

Page 98

landed on the moon — Yuri Gagarin
first man ever in space — Alan Shepard
first American man in space — Neil Armstrong and Buzz Aldrin

Page 99
1. Spirit and Opportunity
2. possible answers: taking photos, collecting air samples, testing the natural elements
3. There may have been water on Mars a long time ago.
4. There may be, or could have been, life on Mars.

Page 100

1,000 — lowest number of moons that Jupiter has
45,000 — number of planet Earths that could fit inside Jupiter
60 — temperature of center of Jupiter

Page 101
Answers will vary.

Page 102

H	G	R	A	N	D	C	A	N	Y	O	N
E	S	E	I	F	B	C	W	I	Y	K	Z
A	H	D	Q	S	X	C	A	E	N	M	T
L	P	U	Z	C	T	O	N	Q	H	A	U
U	S	A	Y	A	N	R	U	I	N	A	U
H	E	X	Q	E	I	D	R	S	K	Q	U
E	B	A	Y	N	U	O	F	Y	E	T	N
A	L	O	U	C	S	R	T	E	A	I	N
O	O	M	U	E	W	G	U	Y	T	N	V

Page 103
1. The coral is sharp.
2. One fish is yellow and black. Another fish is shiny and silver.
3. The stingray is flat, gray, and brown.
4. to get a closer look at the habitat

Page 104
1. vary
2. average
3. earth, atmosphere

Page 105
1. snowy
2. There will be no school because of all the snow.
3. They are very happy and grateful.
4. shining

Page 106
1. whiteout
2. visibility
3. snow
4. freeze
5. wind

Page 107
1. He is not sure if he should keep skiing or stop to help the other skier.
2. Answers will vary.
3. Answers will vary.

Page 108
Drawings will vary.

Page 109
The following should be circled.
1. "Wilson Bentley"
2. "a lacy shape like a star, flower, or fern"
3. "28 degrees"
4. "diamond dust"

Page 110
Stories will vary.

Page 111
1. Warm, humid air from one direction and cold, dry air from the opposite direction meet in a low-pressure area.
2. possible answer: They pick up cows, cars, and sheds.
3. The author feels nervous and frightened.

Page 112
NATURAL DISASTER

Page 113
1. a heat wave
2. Hot weather seems even hotter.
3. when the heat index will be 105 to 110 degrees for at least two days in a row
4. possible answers: health problems, drains energy supply, causes blackouts

Page 114
1. heavy rain and overflowing rivers
2. possible answers: 50 people died, 534 counties were flooded, 55,000 homes were destroyed, damages cost more than $10 billion
3. Midwest rivers
4. bad

Page 115

Page 116

Crossword:
5. d u l l (down: dull)
4. f a s (fast)
6. w e t (down: wet)
2. s h o r t
1. l i g h t
3. g o o d

Page 117
1. New York Harbor
2. Statue of Liberty
3. more than 12 million
4. Answers will vary.

Page 118
Drawings will vary.

Page 119
1. zoh-ol-uh-jee
2. branch of science that studies the animal kingdom, or kingdom animalia
3. zoologist
4. zoo, colleges, laboratories, natural history museums, safari parks
5. possible answers: animal behavior, animals' bodies, animals and their habitats

Page 120
1. evaporation
2. precipitation
3. Water vapor in the air gets cold and changes back into liquid.
4. D

Page 121
1. possible answers: atlas, plane tickets to visit another country
2. Answers will vary.

3. excited
4. go on trips around the world

Page 122
1. a and b
2. opinion
3. fact
4. opinion

Page 123
1. 10 feet high
2. 30 inches in circumference
3. 18 inches
4. 20 to 22 ounces

Page 124
Stories will vary.

Page 125
1. Its saliva has poison.
2. ½ inch
3. It eats the dead body.
4. Yes, because it can already kill an elephant. Elephants are much bigger than humans.

Page 126
1. Scotland
2. 1933
3. a newspaper editor
4. Nessie

Page 127
1. robot
2. sparks
3. hair dryer

Page 128
1. outside of school
2. job
3. less able to do something

Page 129
1. Max is hurting.
2. Max feels better.
3. Answers will vary.

Page 130
1. football
2. David Beckham
3. It's easy to learn and inexpensive to play.
4. organization that governs all levels of soccer

Page 131
1. Sonia was frightened.
2. no
3. Her mouth was numb.
4. She was relieved.

Page 132
Drawings will vary.

Page 133
1. and 2. A person who studies and helps people use the law. A fish.
3. other fish
4. possible answers: females are larger than males, males care for the young

Page 134
Stories will vary.

Page 135
1. nurse

2. Crimean
3. Lady with the Lamp
4. Florence Nightingale

Page 136
1. possible answers: One sock from every pair kept disappearing. He wanted to know if there really was a sock party.
2. He saw the sock escape and discovered the sock party.
3. Answers will vary.

Page 137
fighting a fire, rescuing a cat from a tree, helping at a car accident

Page 138
1. lofts
2. They can find their way home from anywhere.
3. possible answers: Earth's magnetic field, position of the sun, landmarks, smells

Page 139

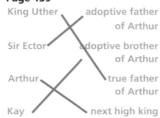

King Uther — true father of Arthur
Sir Ector — adoptive father of Arthur
Arthur — next high king
Kay — adoptive brother of Arthur

Page 140
Stories will vary.

Page 141
1. trolley
2. orange and blue
3. touchdown
4. the best plays of the game

Page 142
1. O
2. F
3. O
4. F

Page 143
1. Alex wants to show him his new talent.
2. He felt sick.
3. Alex is excited.
4. Answers will vary.

Page 144
1. 13
2. Thomas Jefferson
3. August 2, 1776
4. July 8, 1776
5. July 4

Page 145

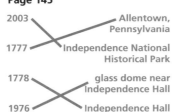

2003 — Independence National Historical Park
1777 — Allentown, Pennsylvania
1778 — Independence Hall
1976 — glass dome near Independence Hall

Page 146
1. She cared for her brothers and sisters. She did many household chores. She made clothes for her family.
2. possible answers: She sewed clothes for her whole family; she earned money by sewing; she sewed other things like curtains; bedspreads, and tablecloths; George Washington chose her to sew the first flag.
3. The modern flag has more stars.

Page 147
1. Billy knows everything about baseball and is a good baseball player.
2. play baseball
3. Billy's father is probably proud of Billy.

Page 148
Stories will vary.

Page 149
padlock, rubber bands, birthday candles, coupons, buttons, matches, tacks

Page 150
1. possible answers: grocer stocking shelves, gas station attendant working pump, school bus drivers traveling routes, man in ski mask creeping along wall of bank
2. superhero
3. Amanda would stop the mugger and return the woman's belongings.

Page 151
Drawings and titles will vary.

Page 152
1. true
2. false
3. true
4. Answers will vary.

Page 153
1. Tommy and Marco
2. the jungle
3. If he doesn't kill his friend, Marco, Tommy will look like a coward.
4. Tommy and Marco are friends, and Tommy isn't allowed to hunt him.

Page 154
1. a
2. a
3. b

Page 155
1. a monster
2. in the closet
3. He feels safe there.
4. under the bed

Page 156
1. rock
2. Paleontologists
3. protected
4. vertebrate

Page 157
1. He was terrified.
2. "They're meat-eaters"
3. "Albert was never one to follow rules"
4. not to wander away from his field trip guide

Page 158
1. characters
2. dialogue
3. author

Page 159
1. and 2.

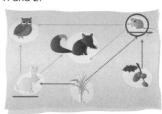

3. Yes, by the owl and fox.
4. Answers will vary.

Page 160
1. Molly McGuire
2. Molly McGuire loves to make cookies.
3. possible answers: measuring, mixing, watching them bake, compliments on her cookies, licking the bowl
4. Answers will vary.

Page 161
Answers will vary.

Page 162

Page 163
1. a prince or leader
2. Doha
3. Arabian Peninsula or in the Middle East
4. Persian Gulf
5. He always interrupts.

Page 164
1. They spell "DOG OUT."
2. Bailey
3. Poetry lines will vary.

Page 165
1. They are white canvas with pink stripes and zippers.
2. They help her run fast.
3. The zippers break.
4. She isn't too upset because she can still run faster than her brother.

Page 166
1. possible answers: being alone, listening to birds, reading, pretending to be someone else, seeing the world from above

2. Up in my tree house
3. Answers will vary.

Page 167
Drawings will vary.

Page 168
1. true
2. false
3. true
4. true

Page 169
1. Y
2. N
3. Y
4. Y
5. N

Page 170
1. The students were not paying attention to her lesson.
2. Ms. Dupree was frustrated.
3. She brought in a dead frog in a jar.

Page 171
<u>3</u> Tadpoles grow legs and their tails begin to disappear.
<u>2</u> When the eggs are ready, a tadpole hatches from each.
<u>1</u> The female frog lays eggs in the water.
<u>4</u> Gills are replaced with lungs, and their hearts, stomachs, and skeletons change.

Page 172
1. possible answers: started in Israel, Jerusalem is holy place, have Orthodox branches
2. Islam
3. Judaism
4. Islam

Page 173
1.

Africa — lion
porch — white sand beach
London — Buckingham Palace
Mexico — package

2. Answers will vary.

Page 174
1. false
2. true
3. true
4. false

Page 175
1. June, 1995
2. the Olympic Games
3. possible answers: skateboarding, BMX, motocross, surfing, snowboarding, skiing, snowmobiling
4. possible answers: he skateboards, he likes Tony Hawk, he likes the X Games

Page 176
1. caring for the presidential pets
2. dog, cat, racoon, pony, sheep, horses, cows, macaw, mockingbird
3. possible answers: Thomas Jefferson, Calvin Coolidge, John F. Kennedy, Theodore Roosevelt, George Bush Senior, George W. Bush, Bill Clinton

Page 177
1. Grace, an eight-year-old girl
2. She is suddenly in a hospital and is expected to act like a doctor.
3. Answers will vary.

Page 178
1. Answers will vary.
2. GRAVITY BRINGS YOU DOWN TO EARTH

Page 179
1. He doesn't think his character is playing well.
2. He was stuck inside the video game. He couldn't kill two enemies at once.

Page 180

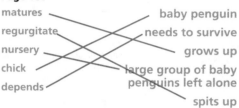

matures — grows up
regurgitate — spits up
nursery — large group of baby penguins left alone
chick — baby penguin
depends — needs to survive

Page 181
1. Her new baby brother is coming home.
2. possible answers: visit from far away, decorate, cooking special meal
3. She feels ignored.

Page 182
1. lead Seamus to a pot of gold
2. He points to a rainbow.
3. Never take your eyes off one

Page 183
1. Stay away from it.
2.

crocodile
pointed snout
freshwater
larger

alligator
rounded
smaller snout
smaller
saltwater

Page 184
1. The sky began to get cloudy.
2. fourth
3. Answers will vary.

Page 185
1. possible answers: elevator, marble, doors, apartments
2. possible answers: elevator, other people in their apartments, knocking, shoes echoing, creaky metal door
3. meatloaf

Page 186
1. to convince people to protect themselves from the sun and to give information about the risks of the sun
2. possible answers: stay out of the sun, wear protective clothing, avoid the sun at peak hours, use sunscreen

Page 187
1. coloring book, crayons, blue ribbon, trophy, two letters
2. two letters, silver ring, lucky coin
3. They laughed.